With Heart and Hand

With Heart and Hand

The Black Church Working to Save Black Children

Susan D. Newman

Judson Press ® Valley Forge

Library of Congress Cataloging-in-Publication Data
Newman, Susan D.
    With heart and hand: the black church working to save black children/Susan D. Newman.
    p. cm.
    ISBN 0-8170-1223-0
    1. Church work with children—United States. 2. Afro-American children—Religious life. I. Title.
BR563.N4N47 1994
259'.22'08996073—dc20   94-39334

Printed in the U.S.A.
95 96 97 98 99 00 01 02   8 7 6 5 4 3 2

Photography credits:
Keith Hadley pages vii, 43, 59, 62; Skjold Photographs, 23.

Contents

Preface

The black church has always been the spiritual and moral heart of our community. Through times of struggle and triumph, progress and peril, the church has been there to ground and inspire us, to provide us with the faith, hope, and services we need to carry on.

Now, with increased violence, drug abuse, homelessness, and poverty, black children and families in America are facing the worst crises since slavery. In the midst of these crises, the black church continues to play a vital role in our physical, moral, and spiritual survival. Indeed, the black church is the only institution with the power and influence to save the black community.

We have many problems to solve. Every 46 seconds of the school day a black child drops out of school. Every 65 seconds a black teenager becomes sexually active. Every 104 seconds a black teenage girl becomes pregnant. Every 11 minutes a black child is arrested for a violent crime. And every 20 hours a black child or young adult under twenty-five dies from causes related to HIV.

These facts, while daunting, can and should inspire us to take positive action. For every problem we're facing, there are a number of solutions at work in our communities. Individuals

and institutions are using creative solutions, mother wit, and solid, traditional values to improve the life chances for black children. And in many cases the black church is leading the way.

With Heart and Hand was written to provide examples of outstanding ministries of the black church across the country that are saving, sustaining, and assuring a future for our black children. These ministries are examples of people living their faith, putting their beliefs into action, and walking the walk. We live in a time when gangs and guns have become surrogate families for our youth, providing a sense of community and protection in unstable, violent environments. We live in a time when adolescent and teenage girls are having babies in hopes of finding love and purpose in their lives. We live in a time when black children, who should be planning what they want to be when they grow up and what kinds of families they want to have, are so accustomed to murder by gunfire that they are planning their own funerals. There *is* hope. There *are* solutions. There is something that everyone can do.

In times past, the adults in our churches and community made children feel valued and important. They took time and paid attention to us. They struggled to find ways to keep us busy. And while life was often hard and resources scarce, we always knew who we were and that the measure of our worth was inside our heads and hearts and not outside in our possessions or on our backs.

The children we take time with today will be our leaders and champions tomorrow. Who knows which little girls we tutor in English today will grow up to be another Toni Morrison or Maya Angelou? Who knows which little boys we mentor in a rites-of-passage program will be the next Thurgood Marshall or Arthur Ashe?

With Heart and Hand describes model programs that are making a positive difference for young people in many communities. These programs provide a blueprint for change and a road map for progress from which we all can learn and benefit. We need to join hands with each other in a massive crusade to "Leave No Child Behind." *

---

* Official slogan of the Children's Defense Fund.

Acknowledgments

This book could not have been produced without the assistance and contributions of the following people:

TaRessa Stovall, who helped write and edit pieces of this book.

Shannon P. Daley.

Lillian Newman and *Joye Brown Toor*, for their love and prayers.

Tuere Saida Harding, a "baby-woman" who helps me "understand the possibilities."

Pamela and Craig, my guardian angels.

Especially my God, who "by the power at work within us is able to accomplish abundantly far more than all we can ask or imagine" (Ephesians 3:20).

Introduction

"Take my hands, and let them move
At the impulse of Thy love; . . .
Take my heart—it is Thine own,
It shall be Thy royal throne."
                                    Frances R. Havergal

With Heart and Hand: The Black Church Working to Save
Black Children is founded on the passage in James 2:26, "For just
as the body without the spirit is dead, so faith without works is
also dead." James was saying that faith without works isn't really
faith. It is dead, and a dead faith is worse than no faith at all.
Faith must work; it must produce; it must be visible. Verbal faith
is not enough; mental faith is insufficient. Faith must move into
action. He emphasizes his point by stressing that Christians
should "be doers of the word, and not merely hearers" (James
1:22).

As Christians, it is not enough to believe in our hearts that
God can do miraculous things to rid our world and communities
of poverty, disease, ignorance, and violence. It is important for
the church to pray faithfully for healing and wholeness in our
families and communities. But equally important is the mission
of the church to work actively to bring about this wholeness. We
must realize, in the words of Annie Johnson Flint, that "Christ
has no hands but our hands. . . no feet but our feet." Therefore,
it is with both heart and hand that the black church works to
save black children.

This book profiles ten successful model ministries of the black church. These churches vary in congregation size, income, and denominational affiliation. Eight of the ten ministries are of entirely black congregations. However, the Montgomery S.T.E.P. Program is a ministry where black and white churches in Montgomery, Alabama, became partners to help black children, and the Sojourners Neighborhood Center is a ministry of "The Sojourners," a multicultural community of faith.

Project SPIRIT and the National One Church, One Child Program are ministries seeking local churches to become a part of their national networks. The Howard Bailey Life Enrichment Program for African American Boys is a ministry of the Penin- sula-Delaware Conference of the United Methodist Church. This program serves as a model for connectional churches (i.e., churches with an episcopal structure) like the African Methodist Episcopal, Christian Methodist Episcopal, and African Method- ist Episcopal Zion.

Each profile shares the ministry's program goals, program description, financial source(s), space and resource needs, vol- unteer needs, and training of volunteers. Each profile ends with an inspiring story about the life of a child who was blessed by that particular ministry. A few have bittersweet stories to share. In an effort to be honest and frank about what happens when we become involved in the lives of other people, I've shared chal- lenges and obstacles that some of the church workers experi- enced while working with families. These challenges range from sexually abused children to threatening adults. It has been the faithfulness of these wonderful people that has enabled them to continue their work in spite of difficulties.

With Heart and Hand includes an article that gives helpful information about how to write a successful proposal requesting grant money to support such ministries. There is a sampling list of foundations that support the black church's work with chil- dren. In addition, this book lists faith-based public policy of- fices, national organizations that work for children, denominational agencies and boards that support ministries with children and families, and a resource list.

It does not take people of great monetary means to perform these ministries, but it does require people of faith and love to minister to the needs of our children and families in crisis. We are reminded by the words of Jesus that ministering to suffering humanity is the most important vocation in life. It is the hope of the faithful community to hear at life's end these words, "'Come, you that are blessed by my Father, inherit the kingdom prepared for you from the foundation of the world; for I was hungry and you gave me food, I was thirsty and you gave me something to drink, I was a stranger and you welcomed me, I was naked and you gave me clothing. I was sick and you took care of me, I was in prison and you visited me'" (Matthew 25:34-36).

1

First Things First

Before your church starts a new program for children, there are a few important assessments that need to be made in order to develop an appropriate, effective, and sustainable new effort:

- Appraise your church's interest and involvement in doing support programs for children.

- Identify your physical, financial, and human resources.

- Assess the unmet needs of children in the vicinity where the church is located.

- Survey organizations and individuals in the neighborhood that are already working to help children.

Conduct a Church/Community Needs Appraisal

To decide which ministry is needed for a particular congregation or community, there are certain questions that should be answered:

- How does your congregation provide suitable educational programs and other activities for children and youths?

- How are children and youths encouraged to participate in the life of the congregation? Is their role primarily as observers?

- Has your congregation offered a program in the past three years to heighten awareness about children at risk and offered ways to minister to such children?

- In the past three years has any adult-education seminar,

1

workshop, or course focused on children's issues and the Christian mission?

- What books or other materials does your church library or resource table offer on children's issues and child advocacy?
- Have the Christian education and mission boards ever worked together on a program or ministry affecting children in the congregation or community?
- Does your congregation conduct a child-care program or an after-school program for children and youths?

Congregation People/Skills Profile

Now that the church is interested in beginning a new ministry for children, a Christian education committee, children and youth ministry team, or a group of interested members needs to meet and make the above-mentioned assessments before deciding which ministry is needed and suited to your particular congregation and community. First, find out the resources available within your congregation. This information may already be available in a database in the administrative office, or the clergy and staff may have access to it. You may want to include a bulletin insert or newsletter article that requests profile information from the membership, with such questions as, Are you willing to volunteer to tutor a child two evenings a week? What skills and abilities can you offer a children's ministry?

When developing the list of people, skills, and interests, be sure to include persons who have professional expertise such as teaching, social work, counseling, health care, music, art, or politics. When screening the availability of the congregation, don't forget to include retired persons and seniors as well as college and high school students who may earn credit for community service projects.

Community Profile

There is no point in reinventing the wheel! Survey the community where your church is located and identify local organizations, agencies, and other churches that already have successful programs for children, such as the YMCA, YWCA, Boys Clubs, and Girls Clubs. You can meet with them and see what you can learn from their efforts, or you can combine resources and people power to have a more effective ministry in that particular community.

Identify key people in your community with whom you want to establish and maintain contact. Consider elected officials, school board members, and persons who have been active in children's issues.

After identifying the community's needs and the congregation's available resources, decide which need matches the majority of your resources. Decide if you have enough resources and support to address the need. This may be a time to seek another church or local agency as a partner in order to successfully meet the pressing needs of the community.

- There may be single parents or teen parents who need support and parenting skills. Congregation members with counseling or social work experience would be excellent to staff a ministry like the Lincoln Adopt-A-Family Program.

- If your church is in a community with a lot of latchkey children who need after-school care and you have members who can volunteer to tutor or teach various subjects, then an after-school program like O.P.T.I.O.N. would be great.

- If your church is in an area where there are female heads of households with male children, a rites of passage/male mentoring program like the Isuthu Institute would benefit the mother and young men. You would need adult men of the church to volunteer their time a few evenings a week plus an occasional weekend to mentor a young boy.

- There may be artists, writers, musicians, dancers, and so forth, in your community who can help children and youth discover a whole new world of culture and the arts through a program like The Love Academy.

As you read the profiles of the following model ministries, think about what your congregation can do for children. Share

these materials with other members and have a special worship
or prayer service where you lift up the needs of children and ask
God to guide you in developing a powerful and faithful ministry
for your community.

Adapted from *Welcome the Child*, a publication of Children's Defense Fund, 25
E Street, NW, Washington, D.C., 20001.

2

National Models

Project SPIRIT

The Congress of National Black Churches, Inc.
Washington, D.C.

"Not by might, nor by power,
but by my spirit, says the LORD of hosts."
Zechariah 4:6

Project SPIRIT (Strength, Perseverance, Imagination, Responsibility, Integrity, and Talent), is a nationally implemented program of the Congress of National Black Churches, Inc. (CNBC), that creates resource centers within the black church to meet the needs of families in the community they serve. Project SPIRIT consists of:

After-School Tutorial Program

Saturday School Program

Living Skills Enhancement Program for Children

Parenting Education Program

Pastoral Counseling Training Program

The program was first developed in 1985 and has been pilot-tested in five black churches in each of three urban sites: Atlanta, Georgia; Indianapolis, Indiana; and Oakland, California. It is often easier to sustain the program when several churches band together; together they can draw on more human and financial resources, and reach out to more of the community than could any one church alone.

Program Goals

The goals of Project SPIRIT are fourfold:

To enhance self-esteem in children.

To improve children's academic performance through positive reinforcement and tutoring.

To help parents become more competent, effective, and loving with their children.

To enhance pastors' assessment and counseling skills.

Program Description

The After-School Program provides a supportive environment of instruction, counseling, nurturing, and group activities to help African American children understand and surmount the stresses they face daily at home, at school, and in the larger community. The program is designed to run for three hours every school day for thirty-six weeks and serves children from six to twelve years of age. Most sites accommodate about twenty children who are divided into at least two groups (6-9 years and 10-12 years).

Instruction takes place through five learning centers:

Communications and Media Arts

In this center children concentrate on the ways modern technology is used to transmit a message. Here they work with video cameras, typewriters, still cameras, tape recorders, and computers.

Math and Science

Children have an uninhibited interest that must be captured and nourished as we teach skills of math and science. This center is the place for textbooks and "manipulables," a terrarium and aquarium, a nature collection, and so forth.

Production Center

The Production Center contains materials children can use to produce a "finished product"—pencils, paint, and paper; clay and papier-mâché; wood and simple woodworking tools; found objects; fabric and embroidery thread. Here children learn the production process: product design, identification of materials, the hands-on activity of creation, revision, and the finished product.

Economic and Resource Development Center

At this center the children learn about jobs and the stock market. They meet with professionals from the community to hear about the world of work, and they plan and carry out their own profitable ventures. This center is also the focus for the program's Ujamaa (collective work) activities.

Distribution Center

In this center the children distribute the products and other items of their creation. Such items can be bought, sold, or displayed. Teachers are encouraged to guide the children in understanding the concepts of retail purchasing, marketing, bartering, and sharing their items and wares.

Each Project SPIRIT after-school component should follow roughly the same daily schedule. Although actual times allotted to each activity may vary somewhat, this simple pattern is the underpinning of the project. For three hours each day the young people enter a "new space" where, in a contemplative and supportive atmosphere, they can release daily stress while sharing who they are and what they have done.

The daily schedule is as follows:

3:30 - 4:00 Greeting and snack

4:00 - 4:30 Welcome circle

4:30 - 5:15 Living enhancement skills activities

5:15 - 6:00 Homework assignments and tutorial assistance

6:00 - 6:15 Ujamaa activity

6:15 - 6:30 Imani circle

The following sections describe what happens in each time slot.

Greeting and Snack

When the children arrive at the After-School Program, they are met and greeted by one of the adults. As the first person the children see each afternoon, the greeter has a very important role—his or her manner may set the tone for the rest of the children's Project SPIRIT day.

Snack time is a time of transition, and it allows the children and adults to bond. The After-School Program offers a simple, healthy afternoon snack, something to tide the children over from lunch at school to dinner at home. Often the volunteer who serves as the "meeter and greeter" will have the snack ready when the young people arrive. At other times, it may be possible for adults and children to prepare the snack together. Program staff should avoid foods that are high in sugar and fat or that have chemical additives because they lead to poor health and negative behavior.

Welcome Circle

Ritualism has been the cornerstone of African American life, and the program draws on this rich heritage, especially in the activities that begin and end the Project SPIRIT day.

The Welcome Circle takes place in the large, central family and community area and serves as a kind of opening exercise for the program. Each day 5 to 10 minutes of silence allow all participants to reflect on the past events of the day and direct their energies toward tasks that remain. The group joins in singing "Lift Every Voice and Sing" or some other inspirational song. There may be prayer, or everyone may consider a proverb. The group may wish to develop its own special opening phrase. Together the group recites its own pledge of affirmation.

Each day the Welcome Circle activity should include a discussion of an aspect of African American history. The children are encouraged to share with the group their experiences and feelings. One activity that can be very meaningful is to have the children introduce themselves, one at a time, by stating their own full name and then identifying themselves through their parentage. For example: "My name is Dorothy S. Jackson, daughter to Curtis and Zilah Jackson, granddaughter to John and Sarah Jackson on my father's side, and granddaughter to Joanne and William Turner on my mother's side." The children continue reciting their lineage as long as they can, and then finish their introduction with a brief stanza from a Langston Hughes poem.

Of course, the children can use another stanza or a proverb of their choice. Use of a speaker's staff adds weight and importance to what each person says (and contributes to order, as well). Each person holds the staff while speaking to the group and then passes it to the next speaker with a word of affirmation. The children design and make the staff the group uses.

Before leaving the Welcome Circle, the group previews the activities scheduled for the rest of the afternoon.

Living Enhancement Skills Activities

These skills activities take place in the various centers of the after-school component. Following the Welcome Circle, each child selects, or is given, a center assignment. For the next 45 minutes or so, the children work on an area relevant to life and to talents and skills they may have that need developing. It is important for the teacher to be an active guide to the children, creating a balance between free choice among centers and encouragement for the skills they need.

Homework and Tutorial Assistance

A purpose of Project SPIRIT is to assist children with their homework without excluding their families from the process. Time is provided for the children to work on their homework, but the parents' role is encouraged by allowing the children to complete unfinished homework at home. The materials the children need for their homework assignments are available, and adults are ready to explain and assist as necessary. However, the homework time should not be extended if the children do not finish. The other aspects of the program are too important to be slighted, and children can (and should) finish their homework at home.

All children must bring books whether or not they have homework to do. Those who have no homework assignments or who have finished may read their books, help other students, or work on their Project SPIRIT assignments.

Ujamaa Activity

"Ujamaa" is a Kiswahili word that means "collective work." Here it stands for an activity that provides not only individual rewards but also an opportunity for cooperative action as a group. The focus here is on economic development, so the activity will be centered in the Economic Development Center. Every day the children receive "tokens" for participating in specific aspects of the program: for example, one red token for attending the after-school component and two green tokens for completing at least one homework assignment. The tasks to be rewarded and the specific rewards offered may vary at different sites. The tokens may be plastic disks, or they may be as simple as rectangles cut from construction paper.

Each day the children deposit their tokens in the "bank." The "banker" of the month, a youngster elected after making a 1- to 2-minute campaign speech, accepts and records all token deposits, helped by a teacher or volunteer. The banker and the adult total the deposits on Friday one week and on Thursday the next week. That second week, Friday is "payday."

On payday the children may withdraw their tokens from the bank and use them to purchase special treats. Sometimes a special snack (homemade cookies or muffins, for example) is offered for sale. Sometimes the children can purchase unusual pencils, popular party favors, stickers, or even extra computer time. Several children who wish to work on a computer project together may pool their tokens and buy a large block of computer time. The possibilities are as varied as the individual Project SPIRIT sites and as the imaginations of the young people.

Imani Circle

"Imani" is a Kiswahili word that means "faith." Gathering in the Imani Circle is the last activity of the day, a final moment for spiritual nurturing. The group may consider a rhyme, poem, or story related to the Living Enhancement Skill activity. Any announcements may be made. Before leaving, the group again recites its pledge of affirmation.

Financial Resources

When a new expansion site for Project SPIRIT has been identified the church(es) interested in participating make individual contributions from $500 to $1,500 to a local account, which goes to fund the development of that particular site.

Monies are needed to purchase supplies and provide stipends for the teachers and volunteers who work with the children.

Space and Resources Needed

The participating church must be able to provide space for twenty to thirty young people and adults. The room(s) will need blackboards, bookcases, tables and chairs, storage space, and so forth. Churches should be advised that local ordinances may mandate certain features, such as the number of square feet per person, access to restroom facilities, and the presence of fire doors. Staff should check with local authorities about specific code requirements.

Ideally the host church will be conveniently located so that most of the children can walk there easily after school. For children who need transportation, the church should provide a bus or van and a responsible driver. Churches are encouraged to be creative in addressing transportation needs while ensuring the safety of the children. A church officer should research legal liabilities involving the transportation of children.

Volunteers Needed

Personnel include at least two teachers per church, and five volunteers who prepare snacks, provide transportation, meet and greet children, and tutor.

Training of Volunteers

The Congress of National Black Churches (CNBC) provides mandatory training for all people involved in the after-school component. Each local site selects Project SPIRIT teachers, who travel in August to spend three to five days at the Project SPIRIT National Technical Resource and Training Center. There they receive intensive training in Project SPIRIT's philosophy, curriculum, and procedures. Project SPIRIT's team of trainers are professionals skilled in curriculum development in the fields of math, science, early childhood education, arts and crafts, communications, child psychology, and psychotherapy. On their return to the local site, trained staff set up two-day workshops to train the local site personnel.

The training for site coordinators, teachers, and volunteers centers on four areas:

administration and coordination of sites;

teacher training and motivation;

curriculum implementation; and

evaluation instrument administration and reporting.

Teachers, in particular, are taught not only how to implement the curriculum but also how to encourage problem solving rather than conflict. They are equipped to teach principles of positive human interaction and to help students reach their full potential. Volunteers, who may be called on to act as substitute teachers, are required to take the same training. One teacher from each site is trained in conducting student evaluations.

Each person who successfully completes the training receives a certificate from the national office. Annual recertification is required.

Regional Advisory Committee

A Regional Advisory Committee is a group of concerned individuals who agree to serve as advisers to the project effort. They usually serve as volunteers, but if the budget permits, they may receive some compensation. Program personnel should be able to look to the advisory committee for technical, financial, organizational, and other important program advice. By representing many community interests, the committee can provide key program sanction and support. A well-constituted advisory committee might include:

a representative from the local school system;

a member of the business community;

a local bank officer;

a representative of the local media;

pastors of two participating churches;

one or more Project SPIRIT parents;

a local political representative; and

a representative of the community.

The committee should meet quarterly and whenever important policy issues need to be considered. Out of consideration to the committee members, meetings should be held in a convenient location and kept as productive and to-the-point as possible.

Pitfalls

Identifying adequate financial support poses a problem. The program operates primarily in inner-city churches in low-income communities, and oftentimes the churches are unable to provide operational dollars. CNBC has begun the formation of fund-development training for its Project SPIRIT churches to assist them in the identification of operational dollars and the eventual incorporation of the program into church budgets.

Advice

Those who are serious about making a difference in the lives of others are encouraged to be very clear in the identification of goals and objectives and to remain true to those goals and objectives. Impart wisdom and build foundations upon which our children and their families may stand and grow.

It Works!

Mydia Prevost came to Project SPIRIT—California in 1987, its second year of operation. A warm, delightful child, she brought with her the curiosities and smiles of any nine-year-old. She also brought with her the challenge of living with a very rare illness.

When less than a year old, Mydia was diagnosed as having Ondine's Curse. Ondine's Curse received its name from the folk story of Ondine, a German water nymph who invoked a curse upon her jilted husband so he would forget to breathe when he fell asleep. Children like Mydia are all right when awake but fail to breathe when they fall asleep. At the time of her diagnosis only eight infants in the world had been diagnosed with this mysterious disease. A great deal of Mydia's early life was spent in the hospital. She had a tracheostomy and now wears a trachea device which she will have to wear for the rest of her life. She still is required to sleep with oxygen at night.

While participating in Project SPIRIT, Mydia lived up to the sparkles in her eyes. The program was her introduction to her cultural history, and she became enamored of the richness of the past. She did her own research and read endlessly to learn as much as she could about her African American heritage.

Mydia often told the Project SPIRIT staff and her friends at Amos Temple CME Church, "Mrs. Cornelius and Mrs. McNeil are my best friends and role models. They always make me feel important and tell me to strive to be the very best I can be."

After reaching age twelve (the current age limit for program participation), Mydia continued to come to Project SPIRIT to tutor the younger children. Her desire to remain a part of the Project SPIRIT family was obvious and heartwarming. Little did the staff know, the challenges of Mydia's life were just beginning to unfold.

In 1990 Mydia experienced three tragedies. She lost her maternal grandmother, who had been a major support to her, her sister, who had sickle cell anemia, and her mother. Project SPIRIT was there to help her through these crises. In August 1993, Mydia was temporarily placed in a foster home in Hayward, California, and was no longer able to continue her participation in Project SPIRIT.

Despite her personal traumas, Mydia remains strong in her faith in God and herself. Presently a high school tenth grader in Hayward, California, Mydia calls periodically to let her Project SPIRIT family at Amos Temple CME Church know how she is doing. She has set a long-term goal to become a lawyer, and according to Mrs. Cornelius, "I know Project SPIRIT influenced her decision; she always worked hard and always gave serious thought to the future."

Mydia has joined the Amos Temple CME Church family, where she participates in the youth choir and attends services when she can. For Mydia Prevost, CNBC's Project SPIRIT made an enormous difference.

Contact:

Project Director
Congress of National Black Churches, Inc.
1225 Eye Street, Suite 750
Washington, DC 20005-3914
(202) 371-1091

Project SPIRIT Churches

California

Amos Temple CME Church
Beebe Memorial CME Church
Cornerstone Baptist Church
Cosmopolitan Baptist Church
Downs Memorial UME Church
Greater St. Paul Baptist Church
Phillips Temple CME Church
Stewart Memorial CME Church
Trinity Missionary Baptist

Georgia

Amanda Flipper AME Church
Bethlehem Baptist Church
Bolton Street Baptist Church
Cathedral of Faith Church of God in Christ
Central Baptist Church
Ebenezer Baptist Church
First African Baptist Church
First African Baptist Church of East Savannah
First Bryan Baptist Church
First Tabernacle Missionary Baptist Church
Greater St. Paul AME Church
Holy Spirit Lutheran Church
Mt. Moriah Baptist Church
Royal Church of Christ
Second Bethlehem Baptist Church
St. James AME Church
St. Paul CME Church
Townsley Chapel AME Church

National One Church, One Child

Tallahassee, Florida

*"Then the king will say to those at his right hand,
'Come, you that are blessed by my Father, inherit
the kingdom prepared for you from the foundation
of the world;... for I was a stranger and you welcomed me.'"* Matthew 25:34-35

One Church, One Child is an adoption program that works
through black churches to locate adoptive families for black
children in need of permanent homes. This ministry was founded
in 1980 in Chicago, Illinois, by Father George Clements, an African
American priest in the Catholic church. The basic principle of the
One Church, One Child program is to find at least one black family
per black church to adopt at least one black child. The program is
now replicated in thirty-three states throughout the country.

Program Goals

To facilitate a national appeal to recruit black adoptive and
foster families for black children.

To provide a national approach to reduce the length of stay
of black children in foster care who are available for
adoption.

To develop a national awareness campaign to educate the
nation of the disproportionate representation of black children in foster care.

To secure a national mandate that provides adequate permanent funding for a national office.

To establish a national clearinghouse to document the number of black children placed for adoption and those still
available for adoption.

To develop a national consortium for the provision of training
and technical assistance for black churches.

To develop a national resource lending library.

To develop a national corporate public/private sponsorship
division.

To develop a national clergy bank.

Program Description

Historically, the black community has taken the responsibility for its own whenever necessary. However, today many black children do not have traditional family support and become caught up in the foster-care system. If black children continue to be raised by the state, they will not receive the quality family care and guidance that has been the cornerstone of the African American community.

The objectives of the One Church, One Child program are:

To familiarize black congregations with the children waiting to be adopted.

To identify in each church black families willing to adopt.

To educate the black community about the need for adoptive homes and about current adoption procedures.

To provide support services to adopting black families and children through training, communications, and location of services.

To decrease the amount of time black children are in foster care waiting to be permanently placed with families.

One Church, One Child of Florida

Through the efforts of U.S. Congresswoman Connie Meeks (then State Senator for Florida), Florida became the first state in the nation to include the program in its state statutes, Section 409.1755, F.S. The One Church, One Child of Florida program was implemented in March 1988. The 1990 Legislature passed the One Church, One Child Corporation Act, which placed the Florida One Church, One Child program into state law. Being included in the state's statutes gives the program statuatory authority and sets a precedent for partnership of church and state.

One Church, One Child operates in conjunction with the Florida Department of Health and Rehabilitative Services (HRS). There are twenty-three board members throughout the state, representing all HRS districts, and a program director located at HRS headquarters in Tallahassee.

Staff and volunteers go into churches to discuss adoption and the need for permanent homes. These persons serve as liaisons to the child welfare system and the One Church, One Child Board of Directors. After a local church becomes a partner with One Church, One Child, an individual church member is selected to be the program representative for that church and is in constant contact with the One Church, One Child office. He or she schedules seminars about adoption in the local church, disseminates materials in the church, and identifies the needs of a particular child to the congregation. Many churches institute adoption ministries where other members of the congregation volunteer to promote awareness of adoption in the community.

Adoption services are offered through the HRS Children, Youth, and Families program. Full-time adoption counselors located in all HRS districts assist One Church, One Child coordinators in finding permanent homes for children.

One Church, One Child of Washington State, Inc.

One Church, One Child of Washington State came about as a direct result of the efforts of a committee for the recruitment of African American adoptive and foster families—Good News for Black Children (GNBC). On October 6 and 7, 1988, GNBC hosted a breakfast for the African American clergy in the Seattle-Tacoma area and a two-day conference entitled "Taking Care of Our Own" in which Father George Clements was the special guest.

On October 20, 1988, the organizing board, composed of area ministers and a group of members from GNBC, began developing strategies to involve state government. On January 11, 1989, this same group met with a representative from the governor's office and a state administrator from the Department of Health and Social Services about the funding of One Church, One Child of Washington State. By this time, the organizing board of the program had accumulated many hours of volunteer time and office space, supplies, and equipment, and a hotline had been donated by the Greater Glory Church of God in Christ.

One Church, One Child of Washington State was incorporated on March 27, 1989, and in August of that year received full funding from the Department of Social and Health Services. This funded the hiring of two full-time employees, the establishing of a fully equipped office, and the training of individuals to present information about the need for African American adoptive and foster homes for children in the state of Washington.

One Church, One Child of Washington State annually holds a Foster Care/Adoption Fair in the fall; another large event in the spring; regular extended-family parent preparation courses and sibling preparation classes; CPR, first aid, and HIV-AIDS awareness classes; cultural awareness and sensitivity trainings; and various seminars and educational trainings for the purpose of advocacy for all children and specialized advocacy for African American children and support for families.

Volunteers

Individuals from various congregations volunteer their time, talents, and resources to assist One Church, One Child. Roles filled by volunteers include:

Sister/Friend

Description: Work one-to-one with a pregnant female to help her find a doctor, arrange for transportation, find out about Women's/Infants'/Children's Services (WIC), Aid to Families with Dependent Children (AFDC), drug rehabilitation, and so forth. Support her and be a friend to her. Help her understand how to have a healthy baby. Be there for her throughout the first year of the baby's life.

Requirements: Have a desire to work with a woman and love her baby. Be responsible, compassionate, and committed to a minimum of fifteen months.

Child Advocate

Description: Write and call legislative/congressional representatives regarding foster/adoption issues. Serve as volunteer Guardian Ad Litem or Court Appointed Special Advocate. Offer testimony at legislative hearings. Organize members of the congregation to act on behalf of children. Volunteer within the public and private sector to improve the foster/adopt placement system. Work on a statewide "Advocacy Phone Tree."

Requirements: Motivation to work within the system for needed changes and a belief that children are our greatest resource. An ability to acquire and share information about ongoing system reform efforts.

Trainer/Presenter

Description: Establish congregational contacts by presenting the need, answering questions, dispelling myths, and getting interested people to sign up for more information regarding adoption and/or foster care. Promote fundraising; provide public speaking at conferences, meetings, and seminars; provide various One Church, One Child training sessions; work with the congregational liaison.

Requirements: Good public-speaking skills; respect for all faith traditions and sensitivity to the concerns of various ethnic communities; completion of the Presenters Training.

Advice

Many people wonder if they can love a child that is not their own flesh. Others are concerned that at some time in the future the natural parents may claim the child. The church volunteers should be trained to share the following pertinent information with perspective parents. ("You" and "your" refers to the prospective adopters.)

Things to know to be an adoptive parent:

You don't have to earn a high income, although you must have enough money to provide for the basic needs of your family.

You can have children of your own or other adopted or foster children.

In most cases, you must be at least twenty-one years old.

You don't have to own your own home.

You don't have to be married.

You must be in good health.

You can work full-time.

You or your family could have faced serious crises, such as illness, unemployment, or other problems, and still qualify.

Preliminary steps in the adoption process

The following steps generally occur once you decide to consider adoption:

A counselor will be assigned to work with you during the adoption process.

The counselor will talk with you about adoption and provide information covering such things as child discipline and guidance. Time will be spent talking about you and your family. You also will have the opportunity to talk about the child you think would best fit into your family.

Your preparation for adoption will include Model Approach to Partnership in Parenting (MAPP) training and home consultations, which will allow you to have a child placed with you. Physical examinations and background checks are required as part of this home study.

After the preparation and study are completed, you and the counselor will be ready to determine which child would fit best in the family.

A series of visits will be arranged between you and the child to allow the child time to meet and get to know you and your family.

When the planned visits between you and the child are ready to proceed, arrangements are made for the actual move of the child into your home.

Generally the adoption can be finalized about six months after a child is placed with you. The counselor will be talking with you and visiting regularly during this period. Then you and the counselor will go to court, where a judge will declare the child a permanent member of your family.

It Works!

This is the story of Rev. T.R. Walker and Mrs. Gladys Walker and their family, told in their own words.

"We fondly remember the first time that we saw our energetic brood of six children. We thought our days of child rearing were over . . . until one night when we were watching the news. We saw a One Church, One Child announcement asking for families to consider adopting six children who had been abandoned by their drug-addicted mother. The children were separated in several foster homes and seemed so sad. At the end of the taping, we saw the children crying when they had to say goodbye. The next day we saw their picture in the local newspaper, along with another boy who also needed a home.

"It did something inside us, and we felt like we owed life something. We immediately decided to call that telephone number on the news to see if we could adopt them to keep them together, even though we had already raised five children. After going through MAPP training and the home study, the children were placed with us in the spring of 1990, the day before Easter. We were so happy to give them a home. After two months of constant complaining from our son about being the only boy with five sisters, we decided to adopt Martin, the other boy in that newspaper article.

"Well, adjustment was not easy in the beginning. Our baby daughter, Margo, was very sick. Erica had some deep resentment towards her birth mother, and Martin was in therapy and on several medications for hyperactivity. Today we are very proud of their accomplishments. Erica, now thirteen, loves to mother the little ones. Margo, six, is the family clown, and Martin, fourteen, wears a permanent grin and loves math. Our other children are a joy to be around. We cannot remember not having the children in our family. Our seven children just needed someone to love them and provide guidance.

"If we had to do it over again, we would do the same thing. If we had more room, we would adopt more children and give them the love of a Christian home. We love our children very much and they love us. We thank God for the strength that he gave us to do what we did."

You can obtain additional information on the One Church,

One Child of Florida Program by contacting the local HRS district office in your area or by writing to:

National One Church, One Child
1317 Winewood Boulevard
Building 8, Room 312
Tallahassee, FL 32399-0700
(904) 488-8251

Local Church Models

MONTGOMERY S.T.E.P.

(Strategies To Elevate People)
Montgomery, Alabama

*"Train children in the right way,
and when old, they will not stray."*
Proverbs 22:6

The Montgomery S.T.E.P. Foundation was organized in 1986 at the Dexter Avenue King Memorial Baptist Church. The purpose of S.T.E.P. is "to proclaim the gospel of Jesus Christ to the poor by mobilizing the Christian churches in Montgomery, Alabama, to work with the poor and with agencies which help the poor so that people are elevated and poverty eliminated for the glory of God." The S.T.E.P. ministry has received accolades from Montgomery's mayor, city council, chief of police, executive director of the Public Housing Authority, circuit judges, and clergy.

Program Goals

A community needs assessment was done, and the data was evaluated over a six-month period before planning the program. There were many needs of the children and their families who lived in the nine low-income housing projects of Montgomery. These needs were addressed through:

The Summer Youth Program
Life Is a Tu-lane Street

After-School Tutoring Program
Mom's Program
Teen Parenting Summer Workshop
Music Program

Volunteers Needed

The S.T.E.P. program is achieved through the efforts of twenty black and white Montgomery churches from nine denominations. There are over five hundred volunteers working with nine public housing projects.

The program pairs a black and a white church to work together. This team of churches adopts a housing community and works with the children and families who live there. Lee Baugh is the director of S.T.E.P., and Rev. Jane Ferguson is the church social worker at First Baptist Church, South Perry Street, who works closely with the program.

Training of Volunteers

Rev. Ferguson is a qualified social worker and does some of the training. Experts in other disciplines are also brought in to train volunteers. Fifteen hours of training are required for certification. This training focuses on skills needed when working with children from disadvantaged homes, such as how to recognize abuse and the importance of listening to children.

Financial Sources

The ministry is supported by donations from the twenty churches and grants. Most churches now include the S.T.E.P. program as a budgeted item of the church.

Administration of Program

A ministerial representative and a lay representative from each of the participating churches make up the council that meets once a month to take care of the business. All participating churches and agencies that work with S.T.E.P. send a representative to a monthly fellowship breakfast. There they share what they are doing in their particular housing community, and others gain new ideas for implementation at their churches.

Program Description

Since 1986 the Montgomery S.T.E.P. Foundation has:
Organized summer vacation Bible schools in housing communities;
Provided tutors for MacMillan Elementary School;
Beautified the playground at Nellie Burge Community Center;
Organized youth outings to Camp Kiwanis;
Organized fund-raising projects for the resident councils;
Organized youth education programs in law awareness, teen pregnancy, and drug-abuse prevention;
Organized monthly drug-free and "Think Big" rallies in the housing communities;
Provided tutoring for the housing communities' children in S.T.E.P. churches;
Developed "Operation Pride," a yearly competition among the housing communities to improve their community life. The winning housing community nominates a young person to receive a fully paid four-year college scholarship to an Alabama state-supported school.

After-school Tutoring

A white church, First Baptist Church on South Perry Street, has paired with a black church, Hutchinson Baptist Church, to provide after-school tutoring for kids in the Tulane Court housing project. The vans from First Baptist pick up the children after school at the Tulane Court housing project, then deliver some of the kids to Hutchinson Baptist Church and some to First Baptist. They are given dinner and an hour of tutoring. Then they gather as a large group for a Bible story and recognition of the teacher and student of the week. About three hundred children from each of the nine housing projects are tutored every Wednesday night.

The summer program is called "Life Is a Tu-lane Street." S.T.E.P. received a $20,000 Governor's Grant for Substance

Abuse for this program. All of the children who regularly attend tutoring programs are qualified to go to Camp Chandler for one week in the summer. At camp the kids are divided into different groups: a music team, sports team, a Bible group, and a self-esteem building program. Black role models come in and talk with the youth. They have seen plays, gone fishing, visited a weather station, and toured the Space Center at Huntsville, Alabama.

Think Big Program

A significant part of the summer is the "Think Big" program. Bill Gailliard, an inspirational speaker and drug and alcohol prevention counselor from Tuskegee, Alabama, emphasizes to the youth the importance of taking care of oneself. Inspired by Dr. Ben Carson's book *Think Big* (HarperCollins, 1993), Mr. Gailliard's self-esteem building and inspirational program provides an avenue for his messages on health, drug abuse, and gang violence. His 45-minute presentation includes positive chants, cheers and raps that entertain while teaching the value of positive thought and a drug-free life.

As a consultant for the S.T.E.P. program, Gailliard works a circuit of the nine public housing projects to share his "Think Big" message to the kids who live there. Each letter of "Think Big" represents a simple reminder of rules to live by: Thankful, Honest, Initiate, Now, Knowledge, Bible, Improve, God.

Mr. Gailliard grabs his audiences' attention through participation. He challenges the kids to Think Big card games, cheering competitions, and songs. Then he tosses them quick questions and awards Think Big money to those who throw back the correct answers. At the conclusion of his nine-week circuit, the S.T.E.P. churches hold a Think Big Fair where children can spend the Think Big play money they've earned for school supplies and clothes. The churches involved in the S.T.E.P. Foundation donate the supplies. Adult volunteers from the churches serve as shopkeepers.

A Think Big Expo was held August 14, 1993, at the Montgomery Civic Center with over twelve hundred housing community residents present. Twenty booths were staffed by successful black businessmen and businesswomen. Professionals from law, medicine, and the arts were on hand to discuss training, education, and career opportunities in their fields of expertise.

Other booths spotlighted arts, crafts, and activities of the children from the housing communities. The Think Big Expo included a large choir of children who had participated in various summer programs around Montgomery.

Finally, funds from Governor Folsom's High Risk Youth Grant helped bring Dr. Ben Carson, a young black neurosurgeon, to Montgomery where he spoke to over twelve hundred high-risk youth and their parents. Dr. Carson grew up in a housing project in Detroit, Michigan, overcame incredible odds to finish first in his class at Yale and first in his class at the University of Michigan Medical School, and is currently the Director of Pediatric Neurosurgery at Johns Hopkins University Hospital in Baltimore. Dr. Carson's visit was a great inspiration to the hundreds of at-risk children in Montgomery's housing projects.

John Wilson, chief of police in Montgomery, says, "The S.T.E.P. program has done a lot in giving the kids a head start and providing them with opportunities when they enter school and the workplace. These kids traditionally have been disadvantaged, and when you throw them into an environment with other kids, it lowers their self-esteem. They are not able to compete as well and [it] puts everybody at a disadvantage when they graduate because they are not ready to go into the workplace and, therefore, many get into criminal aspects of life."

Chief Wilson, in summing up the beauty of the Montgomery S.T.E.P. ministry, says, "One thing that stands out about the S.T.E.P. volunteers is that they don't wait for the folk to come out. They go into the projects themselves and interact with the people. It's had a very positive effect on not only the crime aspects of the community but also on relations in general between black and white, rich and poor, and the community and the police."

Mom's Program

First Baptist Church, South Perry Street, started The Mom's Program, a self-help group for unemployed single mothers at the

Tulane Court public housing project. Transportation is provided for these mothers to meet every Wednesday afternoon at the church. The program's goal is to help single mothers cope with stresses, such as role overload, joblessness, loneliness, isolation, financial stress, and lack of parenting and interpersonal skills. A major emphasis is to give support, encouragement, and the exchange of information from a Christian perspective. The program involves community agencies in addressing topics for discussion chosen by group members. Topics range from sexuality, death, and dependency to spirituality and self-esteem.

Activities, such as games, refreshments, entertainment, and parties, are held to foster fellowship and trust among the group. Social activities include: Get Acquainted Day Pizza Party, baby showers, monthly birthday parties, personal testimonies from persons who have made it, cultural events, and out-of-town trips. Parenting conferences are also provided. As group members improve their decision making and disciplinary skills and increase their self-esteem and self-control, they move back into the workplace.

Two other churches, Frazer Memorial United Methodist and Trinity Presbyterian, are also implementing "Mom's Programs" in their respective housing communities.

It Works!

Cheryl Plato, a twenty-three-year-old high school graduate, was the first student nominated by the Riverside housing community for the Operation Pride Scholarship.

Operation Pride, a program started in 1988 by S.T.E.P., focuses on raising pride in the community through service projects in all nine Montgomery housing communities. An annual competition was established to promote law awareness, education, community pride, and the development of spiritual and religious programs among youths. The S.T.E.P. Foundation's Board of Directors determines the recipient of this scholarship.

Each housing community documents its service projects in a scrapbook, which is judged by *Chalk Dust*, an educational magazine. The community with the winning scrapbook is able to nominate a candidate for a college scholarship.

In 1988 Cheryl Plato received the first full-tuition scholarship to any state-supported school. She chose to attend Troy State University and major in criminal justice. Cheryl had a "C" average in high school, and graduated from college with a 3.26 grade point average with a Bachelor of Science in Criminal Justice and a minor in Human Service. She completed an internship in August 1992 at the Alabama Department of Youth Services at Mt. Meigs, where she worked with twelve- to seventeen-year-olds in their dormitories. She talked with the youth about self-esteem, self-confidence, and parent conflict. Cheryl is presently pursuing a Master's Degree in counseling at Troy State University.

S.T.E.P. Church/Housing Community Relationships

Housing Community	Church
Riverside	Frazer Memorial United Methodist Church
	Aldersgate United Methodist Church
Cedar Park	Trinity Presbyterian Church
	Lutheran Ministries of Central Alabama
Gibbs Village	First Methodist Church
	Bethany Seventh Day Adventist Church
Smiley Court	Highland Church of Christ
	Memorial Presbyterian Church
	Evangel Temple
Paterson Court	Eastwood Presbyterian Church
Trenholm Court	First Baptist Church, Ripley Street
	St. John's Episcopal Church
	Dexter Avenue Martin Luther King Baptist Church
	First Assembly of God
	Grace Christian Ministries
Tulane Court	First Baptist Church, Perry Street
	Hutchinson Street Missionary Baptist Church
	Gospel Tabernacle COGIC Church
	Evangel Temple

Cleveland Court   Cloverdale Baptist Church
                      Starr Baptist Church
                      Beulah Baptist Church

Richardson Terrace   St. John Episcopal Church

Epiphany Lutheran Church, Freedom Baptist, and Maxwell Airforce Base Chapel also support the S.T.E.P. program in various ways.

Contact:

Director of S.T.E.P.
First Baptist Church
305 South Perry Street
Montgomery, AL 36104
(205) 834-6310

Lincoln Adopt-A-Family Program

Lincoln Congregational Temple United Church of Christ
Washington, D.C.

"Open your homes to each other without complaining. Each one, as a good manager of God's different gifts, must use for the good of others the special gifts he has received from God." 1 Peter 4:9-10 (GNB)

Since 1986 the Lincoln Adopt-A-Family Program (LAAFP) has been "adopting" families, assisting them in their efforts to function more effectively in their daily lives and enabling them to make tangible contributions to their communities. The program began as a collaboration between Dr. Peola Butler Dews, founder of Payoff Inc. (Parents and Youths On Family Functioning), Washington, D.C.'s self-help organization, and Elsie Miller Monroe, a member of the Lincoln Temple congregation. Ms. Monroe shared the idea of an Adopt-A-Family Program with members of Lincoln Temple, and they decided to adopt families living in the area of their church.

Program Goals

The idea behind Adopt-A-Family is simple: A family or an organization vows to provide the support and assistance (not necessarily financial) to help a family achieve its goals. This has been accomplished by church members volunteering to develop and maintain a mentor-type relationship with youth and adult members of the "adopted" families.

While a one-year commitment is the rule, many of the adoptees become an extension of the adopter's own family, and they choose to work together until the adoptee's small children finish high school.

Volunteers

LAAFP, with the aid of 175 volunteers, has served forty-two families in the past seven years. The initial LAAFP staff consisted of members of Lincoln Temple, but as time passed staff were added from other churches. The program is now sponsored by Friends of Lincoln and volunteers from the church.

Financial Resources

The Friends of the Adopt-A-Family program provide financial support through individual donations and fundraisers. They have also received some corporate sponsorship. Every year information is sent to the Friends about the program's progress, with needs and requests for donations made at that time.

Program Description

Persons interested in being adopted complete applications and are interviewed by the LAAFP staff. Applicants are usually referred to the church through a community agency, social worker, or by word of mouth. The staff visits the homes and then decides which families will be adopted.

Both parents and children are helped by their adopters. The adopters work to meet a family's needs and help them solve their problems. If tutoring or counseling is needed, it is provided. Many of the adopters are professionals, with expertise in counseling; otherwise, referrals are made.

One "adopted" family of three (a mother and two children) has come off welfare. The mother has worked for a major utility firm for the past three years. Another mother with three children under age ten once lived in a homeless shelter. Since served by LAAFP, she has moved her family to an apartment, obtained her high school equivalency diploma, become employed as an educational aide by the District of Columbia Public Schools, and entered the University of the District of Columbia.

The adopters submit quarterly reports to keep the program staff informed. Sometimes intervention is needed. "If an adopter comes to the program staff and says, 'I think this is a young child who really needs to be looked at,' then we talk with the family person who heads the household and ask if they will be willing to take a course of action that we suggest. We also confer with the school administrators," explains Ms. Monroe.

Pitfalls

When working with families in crisis, problems do arise. Ms. Monroe shared this story about a situation that could have been worse if the church had not been present in these children's lives.

"We had a mother who we believed was all right. She was referred to us by a social worker in the city. She was always sober looking; however, the house was not always clean. When we first met her she had eleven-month-old twin boys, another son a little older, and two girls, one five and the other six.

"One of the adopters working with the two girls was a doctor. She had the two girls at her house and discovered blood in the underpants of one. She took them to the hospital, had them examined, and found out that they both had been sexually abused. One of the girls said it was their mother's boyfriend who abused them, but she wasn't sure when she was asked to identify him.

"The mother denied the possibility of this, and the Family Child Protection Agency put the children back in [her] house. The adopter said when she looked at those children, they carried facial expressions of adults, but they were only five and six years old. LAAFP staff spoke with the grandmother and she agreed to take custody of the children."

"It is my belief," says Ms. Monroe, "that when you take one child out of a household [and put her] into a new environment, the child changes, she likes what she sees. But when she goes back home, the same problems that she left when she walked out the door are still there. That's why my goal is to work with the entire family in order to save the kinds of lives we hope for."

Advice

If you wish to begin a similar program, begin with a planning committee. As a team, determine the scope, goals, and activities of the program. The planning committee could include a chairperson, secretary, treasurer, and someone who will process the applications and schedule interviews with "adopters" and "adoptees." Agree on the purpose and goals of your program, and create and distribute fliers or brochures to invite parents, seniors, and youth in your community, church members, and other organizations to participate. Hold an orientation session for potential participants.

It Works!

The first person taken into the program in 1986 was a drug-addicted mother of four. Eleven LAAFP staff members worked with her. They told her she had to get treatment. Two weeks later she called from the District of Columbia General Hospital where she had enrolled in the drug rehabilitation program there. It was a fourteen-day program that was not sufficient for her needs. One of the members of Lincoln Temple had worked with a program in New York City, the Addicts Rehabilitation Center (ARC). LAAFP sent the mother there for nine months. During this time, the grandmother of two of the children cared for all four children in the family.

After successfully completing ARC, the mother went back to school and completed her Graduation Equivalency Degree. The LAAFP staff filled in as extended family. One staff member was in charge of the school system, another was in charge of the household, and so forth. Each had a duty, and "we literally brought that family through," says Ms. Monroe.

"We have a fifty-five-year-old grandmother who has eleven adult children, and is a mother again for her six grandchildren due to the varied social problems that have disrupted so many families in our communities. A sorority works with the grandmother. Each child is adopted by a member of the sorority and receives one-on-one attention from an adult, who reports to us any problems. Now the grandmother is studying to complete her GED."

Contact:

Lincoln Temple Congregational U.C.C.
1701 11th Street N.W.
Washington, D.C. 20001
(202) 332-2640

The Isuthu Institute

Fellowship Chapel United Church of Christ
Detroit, Michigan

*"My child, give me your heart,
and let your eyes observe my ways."*
Proverbs 23:26

The Isuthu (EE-SOO-THOO) Institute is a rites-of-passage/male responsibility program. It is coordinated by men of the James E. Wadsworth, Jr. Community Center and Fellowship Chapel in Detroit, Michigan, and designed for Afrikan [the Institute's preferred spelling] American males ages six to eighteen who reside in Wayne, Oakland, and Macomb Counties.

"Isuthu," which means coming into manhood, is a rite of passage of the Xhosa people of southern Afrika. Its purpose is to introduce adolescent boys into the responsibilities of manhood. In this ceremony, all men in the tribe come together in celebration of the maturity of a particular young man or a school of young men who are about to cross over into the next phase of their lives.

The concept of Isuthu was adapted by Rev. Wendell Anthony, the pastor of Fellowship Chapel United Church of Christ, in 1979 and has been developed through the dedicated work of Christian men in the years that have followed. The program takes approximately eight months to develop and implement.

Program Goals

The Isuthu Institute strives to help a young man develop spiritually, culturally, mentally, morally, and physically. This is done through volunteer mentorship, comprehensive programming, and parental involvement and cooperation. The Isuthu Institute encompasses physical training/fitness, learning principles, community service projects, field trips, parental meetings, a drill team, and a five-day summer institute held outside of Detroit.

Program Description

Isuthu young men are divided into three groups, referred to as "nations." The **Fante** (6-10 years), **Ga** (11-14 years), and **Ashanti** (15-18 years) nations are named after Afrikan tribes. Each group participates in age-appropriate activities.

In order for a boy to advance from the **Fante** nation to the **Ga** nation, and from the **Ga** nation to the **Ashanti** nation, he must demonstrate his understanding and mastery of the seventeen principles listed below, and how each principle relates to home, family, church and spiritual development, school, community, and membership in the Isuthu Institute.

- Responsibility
- Obedience
- Study and Work
- Goal Setting
- Respect
- Love
- Worship
- The Golden Rule
- Budgeting

- Leadership and Service
- Cooperativeness and Team Work
- Perseverance
- Prayer
- Economic Development
- Right and Wrong
- Faith
- Afrikan/Afrikan American History

In addition to learning and demonstrating mastery of the seventeen principles, boys in each nation must also conform to a dress code. All men and boys attending Isuthu functions are required to dress in Isuthu uniform, which consists of hard-soled polished shoes (no gym shoes), Isuthu shirts, dark slacks (no blue jeans), jackets and coats (neatly hung up during meetings), insignias and pins appropriate to the uniform, no jewelry, and no caps unless related to the Isuthu uniform.

Young men are evaluated by the Isuthu Institute Council of Elders, a group of men aged fifty and older who represent a large cross section of positive and productive living. These accomplished men also developed the seventeen Isuthu principles and serve as counselors when needed.

The ultimate goal of the Isuthu Institute is to take a young man of six, and over a twelve-year period, provide him with the knowledge and values necessary to become a positive adult male role model within the Afrikan American community. When a young man reaches the age of eighteen and has met all necessary requirements, the Isuthu Ceremony is given in his honor. Each young man who completes the Isuthu Institute has learned to love, respect, and educate himself. He is knowledgeable in Christian teachings, his cultural history, his present reality, and his future plans. He was born to life a male, but learned through Isuthu what it takes to become a man.

Volunteers and Resources

Volunteers who are committed to a long-term program were recruited from the church. Volunteers were trained by observing Isuthu Institute operations for a period of three months and then began working within the program in an area of their interest. Professional expertise as it related to manhood development was not required. Volunteers from various professions lent their expertise when needed.

In order to implement the program, a dedicated facility is needed. Materials of the Isuthu Institute need to be displayed at all times. Through the church and community awareness and support Isuthu is able to receive monies and equipment.

Pitfalls

The Isuthu Institute experienced a shortfall of volunteers to work with approximately 150 to 200 young men. This resulted in limited interaction between the adult mentors and young men between planned weekly activities. In addition, the home situations of many of the young men undermined their positive experiences with their Isuthu mentors.

Advice

Take time to think and plan carefully. Don't ever lose faith in your ability to impact young people. Make your efforts part of your lifestyle.

Creed: We Are Isuthu!

We are Isuthu!
Coming from what we are to what we hope to become
Men endowed with a godly spirit
A strong healthy body
And an excellent mind forever searching for knowledge
We are Isuthu!
We know that knowledge will take you where you have to go
but standards and values will keep you there once you have
    arrived
We are Isuthu!
Sons in the Afrikan Diaspora
Descendants of kings and queens, farmers and builders
The inheritors of a golden past and an unlimited future
We are Isuthu!
We stand on principle and not popularity
Knowing that none are great but God
And those who wish to be great must first be a servant of
    others
We are Isuthu!
Knowing that we have a responsibility to someone other than
    ourselves
Knowing that we must not forget from where we've come
Knowing that we must work and pray to get where we have to
    go
We are Isuthu!
We know that we are born in life a male
But we must learn in life what it takes to become a man
We are Isuthuuuuuuu!

Standards of Conduct

Members of the Institute:
  Do not fight or incite fighting.
  Do not report to the Institute while under the influence of
    intoxicants.
  Do not use illegal drugs or narcotics.
  Do not gamble or use illegal gambling devices.

Do not violate common decency or morality in conduct. Always strive to maintain excellence in job performance!

It Works!

Kwame (not his real name) is a ten-year-old self-proclaimed "miracle child." Born about two months prematurely, he was not expected to live past his first days of infancy. Kwame was abandoned by his mother at the age of six and has been raised by his grandmother ever since.

When Kwame came to the Isuthu Institute, he was a young man lacking many basic necessities. His vision required corrective eyeglasses, but his grandmother couldn't afford to buy them. He had few items of clothing. He longed to be loved and had very low self-esteem.

Several mentors within the Isuthu Institute personally adopted Kwame. They bought him glasses and clothing. Kwame developed many father-son types of relationships and has grown to understand and appreciate expressions of love and caring. Formerly very shy and withdrawn, Kwame now has a hug ready for his Isuthu men.

As a result of his outstanding academic performance and consistent involvement in the Isuthu institute, Kwame has, for the last three years, earned the right to attend the annual Isuthu Summer Institute at no cost to his familiy. His participation in the Isuthu Drill Team, a vehicle that promotes discipline, self-control, and critical thinking, has been instrumental in his rapid maturation and development.

Kwame's story reminds Isuthu mentors that their efforts are not in vain. He is and will continue to be a wonderful example of what Afrikan American men with a Christian mission can do to raise up the children of their communities.

Contact:

James E. Wadsworth, Jr. Community Center
19621 West McNichols Road
Detroit, Michigan 48219
(313) 531-5980

The Love Academy

Love Zion Baptist Church
Columbus, Ohio

"The righteous walk in integrity—
happy are the children who follow them!"
Proverbs 20:7

The Love Academy, a nonprofit corporation, is a national demonstration model in learning for young children ages three to five and school-age youth ages six to sixteen. The innovative aspect of the program is its emphasis on the cultural arts.

Program Goals

The goals of the Love Academy are to improve the well-being of children and youths and to establish a lifelong love for learning. The target population for the Love Academy draws from low-income African American children living in the immediate neighborhood of the facility; African American children of diverse socioeconomic backgrounds who live throughout the city; and children from multicultural backgrounds through employer child-care benefits provided by both Park Medical Center and Grant Hospital Medical Center.

Program Description

Serving primarily an African American population, the Love Academy emphasizes learning in academics, ethics, and cultural arts and operates through preschool and after-school programming. Dr. Jesse Wood, executive director and program designer, and Joan Wood, executive administrator and artistic director, provide training and technical assistance through the pilot site and conferences. Members of the Love Zion Baptist Church volunteer their time and talents and donate supplies as well as money to support this ministry.

The Cultural Arts Enrichment Institute is an after-school, hands-on arts program, serving over one hundred school-age children annually. Program components include:

- a music and performance program with Opera Columbus;
- a multimedia visual arts program with the Columbus Museum of Art and resident artist, Richard Duarte Brown, including an annual exhibition of student works;
- a theater arts program; and
- a dance program with Myrna Russell, former Broadway performer and dancer with the Alvin Ailey Dance Company.

In collaboration with Opera Columbus, the Love Academy students learned about opera both as spectators and participants. The final portion of their three-month experience was the production and presentation of an opera, "A Muskrat Lullaby." An opera such as this will be presented each year.

With the Columbus Museum of Art, the Love Academy students studied painting, photograms, and sculpture with prominent African American artists. The students' artworks were displayed at a local gallery and two local banks. Outstanding student artists were awarded scholarship monies for college by the Mays King Endowment. The cultural arts program is sup-

ported by ongoing grants from Bank One Corporation and the
Huntington National Bank.

The Learning Center, a preschool and child-care program for
150 children ages three to five opened in 1994. The objectives
are to teach the children self-discipline, respect for others, and
a sense of cultural history. The program includes:

- an emphasis on development through participation in
  dance, theater, music, and visual arts;*
- academic learning which emphasizes vocabulary building,
  mathematics, science, and computer literacy;
- a spiritual emphasis on ethical living drawn from the
  Afrocentric celebration of Kwanzaa and the seven principles of daily living of Nguzo Saba;
- parent volunteer opportunities and classes in nutrition,
  well-child care, parenting, nurturing, money management,
  and self-esteem/determination.

In February 1993, the Love Academy successfully competed
for and received designation as a "Right from the Start Model
Site" through Action for Children, the largest resource and
referral agency for child care in Ohio.

Financial Resources

Through aggressive recruitment of community leaders in
business, education, social services, and other areas, the Love
Academy has built a collaboration of local people working
together to solve community problems. Financial assistance for
the Love Academy comes from state, federal, and private funding, sliding-scale fees, and a wide-ranging, community-based
collaboration of businesses, schools, social services, arts organizations, health services, and child-care professional agencies.

The Mays/King Endowment Fund provides the Love Academy's older students with financial aid for college. The fund,
administered through the Columbus Foundation, raises money
through patron contributions, art sales, and the Love Academy's
Speakers Bureau, which brings national African American role
models to Columbus.

*Based in part on the nationally recognized primary-school program at the Ashley
River Creative Arts Elementary School in South Carolina.

It Works!

John David Jackson is a nine-year-old African American male, born February 23, 1985, in Columbus, Ohio. John is in the third grade at Fairwood Elementary School. He is the middle child of three children born to Linda and John Jackson.

John has been blessed with an artistic gift, but like many young African American males, he did not have the opportunity to develop it. He would draw at home, and whenever pen and paper were placed in his hands, he could fill his days giving freedom to his artistic mind. When John began participating in the Love Academy programs, he was extremely active and would not focus on the assignment. However, as he worked more with his hands, John began to see how talented he was and what wonderful work he could create.

His talent and hard work won him a first place scholarship in the Love Academy's first visual arts program. John has since become a more focused young man. He was baptized over the summer, and demonstrates a real love for the artistic gift God has given him.

Contact:

Love Zion Baptist Church
1459 Madison Avenue
Columbus, Ohio 43205-1580
(614) 258-2216

O.P.T.I.O.N.

Church of the Redeemer, Presbyterian
Washington, D.C.

*"May our sons in their youth be like plants full
grown,
our daughters like corner pillars,
cut for the building of a palace."*
Psalm 144:12

O.P.T.I.O.N. (Opening Pathways To Infinite Opportunities
Now) is a program designed to provide youths with greater
opportunities for their future. It establishes a partnership between the Young Adults of Redeemer (YAR), who are between
the ages of twenty-two and forty, and Taft Junior High School
students.

Program Goals

The immediate goals are to increase the number of academically successful students, provide positive career options, and
teach skills needed to achieve success. The ultimate goal of
O.P.T.I.O.N. is to provide each student with post secondary
school options. Each student can earn up to five hundred dollars
in college or technical/vocational school scholarship money for
each semester that the student meets the program requirements.

Program Description

To effectively function in the future, YAR feels that our youth
will need certain skills. To develop these skills, O.P.T.I.O.N.
activities assist students in filling an empowering "toolbox."
The "toolbox" includes the following:

- Support System—building a one-to-one relationship with
  a YAR mentor whose current career generally matches the
  student's career goals. The mentor is responsible for seeing
  that the student meets the program requirements.
- Goals—teaching the students how to establish and achieve
  their goals; empowering the students to use determination

and persistence.

- Academic Enrichment—making academic excellence a foundation for future success is the goal. The program offers academic achievement incentives.
- Social Alternatives—offering monthly activities that enhance socialization skills. Each activity is planned by the students, with guidance and support from YAR.
- Responsibility—developing sessions and activities that teach students to take responsibility for their words and actions.
- Self-esteem and Identity Awareness—developing activities and field trips that expose the students to a variety of positive role models, both current and historical, and to various career options.
- Effective Communications—teaching each student intra-group communications skills, the art of networking, and basic public speaking.
- Leadership, Planning, Organization, and Team-building—creating activities wherein each student acts as a group leader, develops a plan, and organizes a team to accomplish a specified task, such as a community service project.
- Helping the "least of these"—developing community service projects that teach students to accept responsibility for helping future generations of youth, the elderly, and others in need.

To qualify for participation, students should meet the following requirements:

- Be currently in the seventh grade.
- Have a recommendation from their junior high school.
- Have a demonstrated ability to strive for academic excellence.
- Have an acceptable attendance record.
- Obtain parental consent.

In order to be a mentor, YAR members must:

- Have a desire to help children improve their lives academically, spiritually, and morally.
- Be able to volunteer at least four hours a week.

- Be willing to engage the youth in conversation around issues like self-esteem, peer pressure, and parental conflict.

In order to provide each qualifying student with a scholarship upon graduation from high school, YAR aggressively participates in various fundraising activities and solicits business and individual sponsorships.

Each semester the scholarship funds are deposited in an escrow account. The appropriate invested escrow funds will be released when the qualifying student graduates from high school and enrolls in an accredited junior college, college/university, or technical/vocational school. The funds will then be deposited at the institution in an account in the student's name.

To earn scholarship deposits each semester, the student, with help from his or her mentor, must:

- Achieve a preestablished academic performance standard. Scholarships are granted on a graduated scale based on academic performance.
- Maintain an acceptable attendance record.
- Maintain weekly contact with YAR.
- Attend one O.P.T.I.O.N.-sponsored enrichment/support session and one social function each month.
- Develop a study plan with a quarterly review by an academic advisor.
- Provide twenty hours of community service or political awareness support each year.
- Plan, organize, and chair one event each year.
- Participate in at least one extracurricular activity each year.
- Prepare and present a speech or participate in other public-speaking activities two times each year.

It Works!

Bonnie Sullivan shares her reflections of how O.P.T.I.O.N. has blessed the life of a child.

"Granted, it had been a long time since I had been in a junior high school, and even longer since I had been a junior high school student, but I thought one needed to behave a certain way in order to ensure graduation. Attending class with books, pens, pencils, and alertness helped from what I remembered. There he was, lacking all of these.

"I first met William when he was a seventh grade student. He attended a parent/student orientation program sponsored by our newly created program, O.P.T.I.O.N. Of the twenty-five students that had been invited to participate, fifteen had shown up. Of those fifteen, only three had parents or guardians with them. William was one of [those students]. His mother wanted lots of information and was excited about his participation. William seemed a little shy and uninterested at the same time, but there was something there that made you want to make sure he was taken care of.

"When I walked into Taft Junior High School for a weekly site visit, I must confess I was a little nervous. I don't remember security guards at my junior high school or kids hanging out in the stairwells in the middle of a class period. Here I was, seven months pregnant, filling in for our on-site coordinator and using (work) leave to do so.

"I found the room where the English II class was being held, and there he was, head down on the desk in the back of the room. It was fifteen minutes into a forty-five-minute class period and the teacher was still trying to begin class. Students were still straggling in. Several students from the program were in this class. Two students asked for a pencil because they didn't have one. I happened to have more in my purse than they had in the room. I asked another (student) where his books were. And then there was William.

"I asked him if he felt ok, and he said yes. I asked him how much he could learn with his head down, and he said he didn't care. I decided that this was not the place to pursue the matter and decided to talk to him at our meeting the next evening. He didn't show up. One of the students said William had been physically threatened by another student and was barely coming to class.

"I called after not seeing him for three weeks, and he agreed to come out for tutoring. He explained that he was about to fail several classes and wanted extra help. Rick, one of our tutors, agreed to work with him individually. Each week from then on William came with books and assignments completed.

"On June 17, 1993, I again found myself taking work leave and going to Taft. This time it was graduation day. I wouldn't miss this one for the world. Eight of the eleven active students in O.P.T.I.O.N. would graduate on this day. As I sat there in the auditorium reviewing the program, I saw the names of three of our students listed for recognition. One of them was William. Here he was being honored a year after the "head down" incident as most improved student. He had managed to turn his failing grades into successes, and his teachers were most impressed with his social skills.

"I know that we can't take credit for it all, but William thinks we helped him a lot. He called several times during the summer and after school began this fall to ask all of the tutors if they were coming back. One thing was for sure, William was!"

Contact:

O.P.T.I.O.N. Program
Church of the Redeemer, Presbyterian
1423 Girard Street N.E.
Washington, D.C. 20017
(202) 832-0095

Sojourners Neighborhood Center

Washington, D.C.

"And the streets of the city shall be full of boys and girls playing in its streets."

Zechariah 8:5

Sojourners Neighborhood Center, a ministry of Sojourners Community Church, is committed to faith imperatives of racial reconciliation, justice for poor people, peacemaking, and spiritual renewal. The Center is located in Columbia Heights, an area of Washington, D.C., whose fifteen thousand residents are mostly low-income African Americans, with a growing population of Latinos.

In August 1975, thirty-one people moved into Columbia Heights to start the Sojourners Neighborhood Center. Barbara Tamialis, co-executive director of the Center, says, "We felt God's call in our life deeply rooted in walking with marginalized and oppressed people—not as solution bearers but as fellow travelers." The now famous quote of Lilla Watson, an Australian aborigine, sums up our calling well: "If you have come to help me, you are wasting your time. But if you have come because your liberation is bound up with mine, then let us walk together!"

The Sojourners began meeting with their neighbors in various homes, in rented space of housing complexes, and in the basement of a condemned building. Eventually they found a burned-out shell of a large house, which they purchased. On Good Friday 1983, they went to settlement with the ten thousand dollar down payment contributed by subscribers to the magazine *Sojourners*.

Program Goals

The Sojourners Center's mission is to work with both children and adults in the community to strengthen the family support base. Individuals are encouraged and empowered to develop God-given gifts in order to have the strength to counter a world too often overpowered by drugs, crime, and hopelessness.

The Center's goal is to increase the self-sufficiency of neighborhood residents by helping them determine directions for themselves and for the neighborhood as a whole. Their work directives are: children's programs, food programs, and M.O.R.E. (Mother's Organized Resources for Empowerment), a parent-support program designed to help mothers on public assistance. Beyond this, the Center works toward being a place where differences of class, race, gender, and culture can be recognized, respected, and reconciled.

Program Description

Each component of the children's program is integrated into monthly themes that seek to build self-esteem among the children through work sheets, field trips, and special activities.

After-School Programs: Study-hall group—forty children work daily on homework, monthly themes, and other special projects. Young learners group—kindergarten through second grade students work daily in a learning environment specifically designed for their developmental level. The young learner's room has a collection of "hands-on" learning materials, including building blocks, art supplies, and dramatic play resources. Monthly educational field trips—museums, plays, etc. Computer learning—the computer lab has six well-equipped computers with over fifty different educational programs. These programs help develop reading, mathematical, spelling, and thinking skills.

Evening Program: Each group activity seeks to assist the children in increasing their ability to grow in self-esteem. These activities include male-mentoring groups (divided into ages ten and up and ten and under), female-mentoring groups (similarly divided), computer learning group, arts and crafts group, drama group, Bible studies group, gospel choir group, creative writing group, recreation/physical education group, and a scientific learning group.

Parent Association Support Group: Parents meet monthly with staff members for mutual support, to talk about the work their children are doing, and to work on developing a partnership that will be empowering to them and their children.

College Scholarships: Sojourners participates in the Free the Children Trust (FCT), a private sector partnership between the business/professional community and neighborhood organizations. FCT works to send inner-city youths to college. Some of Sojourners' children have already been selected as FCT recipients.

Youth Task Force: Sojourners is a member of the Youth Leadership and Academic Development Task Force, a network of twenty-one community centers that are providing educational and other services for at-risk youths in the District of Columbia.

Public Schools: Staff visit area schools regularly to keep in touch with the teachers of children from the Center. SNC participated in discussions between principals, the school board representative for SNC's ward, teachers, and parents about restructuring the school in the neighborhood to better meet the needs of the children.

Summer Program: Each summer SNC has a seven-week program designed around a topical theme:

I Am Somebody (1989)—concentrated on developing self-esteem by helping children identify the many gifts and talents they have. Emphasis was placed on participation in music, storytelling, and the performing arts.

Express Yourself (1990)—focused on expressing the talents and gifts discovered the summer before. During the summer the children designed and painted a mural depicting positive daily scenes and activities from the neighborhood. It now hangs on the side of SNC's building.

Time to Make a Change (1991)—devoted to developing conflict resolution skills and looking for new and constructive ways of expressing anger.

Daily Reading Program (1992)—SNC organized a structured reading program that sought to maintain and sharpen reading skills during summer vacation.

Feeding Families

SNC's food programs are directed and supervised by the recipients of the program themselves. Over sixty volunteers pick up, sort, and distribute food weekly to families in the neighborhood. The food is purchased with money donated from various people specifically for this purpose. Some food is received from the National Capital Area Food Bank.

Food Distribution Program: SNC distributes food to two hundred individuals and families weekly. Food is also delivered to eighty-five homebound senior citizens twice monthly. Half of the food recipients are senior citizens who have worked all their lives but find that they can not get by on meager Social Security benefits. Many other recipients are unemployed and underemployed residents of the neighborhood.

Commodity Supplemental Food Program: SNC is a volunteer site for this federal program and provides monthly food for pregnant women, infants, children under six, and senior citizens. About six hundred individuals are served each month.

Food Co-op: SNC sells a variety of low-cost food as an alternative to the high-priced local convenience stores and supermarkets. The Co-op is open once a week and is available to everyone.

Mothers Organizing Resources for Empowerment (M.O.R.E)

The program's goal is to enable participants to break the cycle of dependence and move toward self-reliance. The basic course is an eight-week series of classes devoted to nutrition education and food preparation along with parenting skills, self-esteem building, personal and professional goal setting, and educational opportunities for job readiness.

Summer Program

The goal of the summer program is to provide forty low-income children and youths with numerous opportunities to build skills that will lead to self-sufficiency. Skills are developed via Afrocentric curricula, tutorial support, a mentor program, field trips, and recreational events. The program is free of charge to parents. However, parents are expected to volunteer a minimum of one hour per month per child to the program and attend all parent-related meetings and events.

Sojourners is committed to training what they call "present day freedom fighters." Sojourners believes that throughout African American history there have been freedom fighters like

Harriet Tubman and Martin Luther King, Jr., who have stood against the forces that threatened to destroy them. SNC holds up freedom fighters of the past and presents them as models for our children today.

During the summer the children:

- study the freedom fighters from every era of black American history to discover the character, motivations, and roles of each one;
- meet present-day freedom fighters—people whose lives are directed by principles of liberation, discipline, and self-development;
- visit places of importance to the black American freedom struggle;
- play, swim, hike, and exercise in safe and beautiful environments;
- participate in experiences with the arts, dance, and drama to help develop their creative abilities;
- are fed healthy meals and encouraged to develop healthy eating and exercise habits;
- visit the library, read, and write to express themselves;
- do service projects to aid those in the neighborhood who have needs;
- take a trip out of state during the last week of the program.

There are also monthly trips and activities for parents.

It Works!

Barbara Tamialis, co-executive director of Sojourners, shares her remembrance of a child touched by Sojourners.

"For several years in the late seventies we operated a child development center in the Clifton Terrace apartment complex in northwest D.C. It was there that I first met Terrell (not his real name) and his mother. Terrell was an angry two-year-old who was very aggressive toward other children and adults, including his mother. He was very much out of control and his mother, a teenager herself, was embarrassed by his behavior and felt helpless to change it.

"After several attacks on other children and staff members, we asked Terrell's mother to come in for a conference. We told her that we would keep Terrell in the program only if she would participate in counseling. She was happy to have the chance both to keep him in the program and to get assistance with the problem. Because she took the counseling very seriously, we began to see rapid improvement in Terrell's behavior. Within a short time he began to be more relaxed, made many friends, and was able to concentrate on learning.

"At age five he enrolled in the local elementary school and continued to participate in programs connected with our center over the years. At times when he was not enrolled in formal programs, we were able to keep in touch with his family because the staff at Sojourners live in the neighborhood where we also work.

"On several occasions, the family underwent trauma related to personal issues, and at these times Terrell would begin to exhibit some of the hostility from his childhood. But his mother was able to step in and set appropriate limits and also seek the support she needed. When Terrell reached junior high school, he began to participate in organized sports, which were a great release for his energy and aggressions. Although his participation in sports teams took him away from our school program, we remained in touch with him and his mother more informally.

"In the spring of 1991, Terrell was granted a college scholarship through his participation at Sojourners. He continues to do well academically, and his mother asks for special help for him when he needs it. He has a mentor who has become a father figure to him and is very committed to his development. Terrell has become a very well-adjusted young man with many hopes and dreams for his future and is on the way to attaining those dreams. His mother has also begun to go to college to pursue her own interests and career. We are very proud of Terrell and believe that his life is testimony to what can happen when parents and community organizations (especially religiously based organizations) become partners in raising the children of our inner cities."

Contact:

Sojourners Neighborhood Center
1323 Girard Street N.W.
Washington, DC 20009
(202) 387-7000

The Glide Educational Center

Glide Memorial United Methodist Church
San Francisco, California

*"People were bringing little children to him in order that
he might touch them; and the disciples spoke sternly to
them. But when Jesus saw this, he was indignant . . . and
he took them up in his arms, laid his hands on them,
and blessed them."* Mark 10:13-14a,16

Program Goals

For more than twenty-six years, Glide Memorial United Methodist Church has accepted and served the addicted and disenfranchised of San Francisco's Tenderloin district and the entire San Francisco Bay Area. Glide remains extremely sensitive to the condition of the homeless, especially among youth. So many homeless youths have little or no hope for any improvement in their condition, suffer low self-esteem and an abiding sense of powerlessness, and define themselves on the basis of the individuals and institutions that have rejected and dehumanized them. A youth's initial experience with Glide can be likened to receiving the support of a Christian family within the comfort and security of the family home. This is especially meaningful to those who have no home and those also without a conventional family.

Volunteers and Financial Support

Glide has provided more than just support and spiritual guidance for these youths. The Glide community, with over 150 volunteers from the church and staff, serves as an extended Christian family. Glide families have provided homes for five homeless youths between the ages of twelve and sixteen, who have made the conscious decisions to leave their homes because of intolerable physical and/or substance abuse. The youths' parents and the Department of Social Services are aware of the arrangement. However, many of the families who have agreed to take care of these youth struggle financially to provide them with even the barest necessities.

Members of the church serve as members of the advisory board and coordinate activities for youths. The ministry is financially supported by private donations and grants.

Program Description

The Glide Youth Ministry is trying to foster long-term benefits for these youths. Through the Computer Peer Tutoring Program, they are trained to tutor other youths in computers. It is important that these youths become computer literate and pass this essential skill on to others.

The Computer Peer Tutoring Program utilizes Glide staff, a computer consultant and the peer tutor to meet the comprehensive needs of the students. The computer consultant teaches computer skills, trains peer tutors in tutoring skills, and supervises the one-to-one interaction between peer tutor and student.

Peer tutors earn a weekly motivational stipend of twenty dollars. This promotes responsible attitudes toward prompt, regular attendance and a professional attitude. The Peer Tutoring Program instills good work ethics, such as following through on assignments, accepting consequences for actions taken, and being responsible for another person.

Glide's experience with these five youths convinced them that living with other families is beneficial. Considering their previous environments and histories, these kids have exceeded the expectations of society. They have avoided the pitfalls of jail, drug abuse, and pregnancy. They regularly attend school, actively participate in Glide programs, embrace Christian values, and exude an enthusiasm in their everyday interactions that was barely palpable before.

As an adjunct to the Peer Tutoring Program, Glide has an incentive plan for those youths who have been identified by staff as having serious potential for high-risk behavior. Many of these children are currently homeless or in foster care, abusive homes, or volatile situations that do not support their emotional, spiritual, and intellectual growth. The Glide staff has extensive experience with such youth and are often in close contact with their teachers and/or parents.

The goal of the Computer Peer Tutoring Program is to provide homeless and near-homeless youth with the opportunity to build self-esteem, develop Christian values and spirituality, make positive choices, understand their feelings, accept responsibility for their actions, and earn an allowance or incentives for good behavior.

The incentive plan revolves around a system where points are given for school attendance, citizenship, improvement in grades, and participation in the program. Essential items, such as school supplies, clothes, shoes, and backpacks, can be acquired by youths who have earned the necessary points.

By making the choice to leave their homes—be it with parent(s) or foster parents—these youths need an alternative support system that provides an extended Christian family environment, caring relationships, basic services, and educational opportunities. Through the Peer Tutoring Program, Glide provides a positive relationship for these youths, while insuring that their struggle towards self-empowerment does not go unrewarded.

The Glide Children's Program inspires children to discover their inner miracles. There are currently 145 children and youths, ages two to eighteen, enrolled. The ethnic breakdown is roughly 65 percent African American, 20 percent Asian, 13 percent white, and 2 percent Latino. Many of these children are

high-risk, inner-city youth who have never known familial stability or economic security. The Glide Children's Program acts as "home" for these children, providing them with a myriad of choices where before they had none. Most of the participating parents are enrolled in other Glide programs, such as the Recovery program and/or the Jobs Training Program.

For school-aged youth, there is an extensive after-school tutorial program, which currently has sixty-five participants. Volunteers, under the guidance of the program director, work one-on-one to provide academic assistance and/or encouragement.

For youths who have additional needs or particular problems, there is the Circle-of-Friends support group. An average of fifteen youths share their troubles and concerns in group meetings, which are held in a circle and led by a trained adult volunteer.

For teens there are a number of programs. The Teen Club has twenty-five young people enrolled and focuses activities around spirituality and values clarification. The Teen Parent Group offers parenting skills courses, support groups and vocational enhancement training.

The Glide Children's Program also has many creative and recreational programs. The Girl Scouts/Girl's Club provides weekend activities and currently has thirty-three young women enrolled. For young males there is the Boy's Club, which has twenty enrolled, and includes weekend sports activities. There is also a theatre group, sponsored by American Conservatory Theatre, which offers weekend musical theatre classes.

The Glide Children's Summer Recreational Program provides scholarships for youth to attend summer camp and experience life outside of urban areas. Other daily activities include trips to museums, historical sights, and landmarks.

It Works!

Amber is fifteen years old, although she looks a lot older. She became a member of the Glide family when she was nine. Her mother, Brenda, is a prostitute who has AIDS and blames her troubles on Amber. But Amber is devoted to her mother and wants to take care of her. Her mother's house was under surveillance for drug trafficking, and the police once arrested Amber in school in front of other students and teachers, having mistaken Amber for Brenda. Brenda's house and friends present a dangerous and negative environment for a young girl in puberty. Amber's choices in life can go either way, depending upon who influences her.

Joyce Hayes, the program director, has worked hard on Amber's behalf. Amber is now in the care of a loving Christian family from the church and is attending school regularly. She is now able to reclaim a lost childhood and begin living the life of a teenage girl, instead of being the caretaker for her mother.

What is difficult for children like Amber is that they are sometimes expected to make important decisions about their lives and their future, at an age where children in stable conditions just go to school, play, and otherwise trust their responsible parents to make those decisions. This responsibility can be too big, adding to the already big enough confusion and turmoil in their lives. Joyce said, "Sometimes they just cannot be spared. All we can do is offer our best advice and undivided attention and let them feel our dedication, that they might put their trust in us, confide in us, and let us help them. Through our counseling, we hope to better their judgment, that they may make the right choices."

Contact:

Director, Children's Program
Glide Memorial United Methodist Church
330 Ellis Street
San Francisco, CA 94102
(415) 771-3724

The Howard Bailey Life Enrichment Program for African American Boys

Peninsula-Delaware Conference of the United Methodist Church

"Yet it was you who took me from the womb;
*   you kept me safe on my mother's breast.*
On you I was cast from my birth,
*   and since my mother bore me you have*
*   been my God.*
Do not be far from me,
*   for trouble is near*
*   and there is no one to help."*
                                        Psalm 22:9-11

Program Goals

The Howard Bailey Life Enrichment Program for African American Boys was designed to put black boys in touch with positive African American male role models. The program seeks to reverse some of the negative images, dilemmas, and consequences of living in what has become a hostile enviroment for many African American men. Its goal is to direct a young boy's life through claiming and reclaiming traditional African religionism, history, culture, and reverence for African heritage and ancestry.

Program Description

This ministry engages African American boys in various settings through examining history, literature, and the media. The program is based on four ideals:

- Reidentification of the positive aspects of African American community life to counter negative media images.
- Reclarification of one's own station in life.
- Redefinition of the individual's place in God's created order.
- Reaffirmation of self.

The Bailey Program is conducted in a fun and safe environment. Camp Pecometh is the ideal setting for the program. The boys attend the camp one weekend in May, a week in June, and a weekend in October. There are fifty boys in the program. Twenty-five boys in the fifth and sixth grades are in the Marcus Garvey Group, and twenty-five seventh and eighth graders are in the George Washington Carver group.

Components of the program include recreation and team-building activities, service to the church and community, educational opportunities, field trips, activities with parents, awareness of self, keeping a journal, pastoral support and encouragement.

Volunteers

Each boy is paired with a "presiding adult" who mentors him. The presiding adult is expected to befriend the boy and his family; be a trusted listener who is sympathetic to the boy's situation; encourage the boy in school, family, and peer group situations; be responsible for his transportation to and from camp; arrange one or more educational/recreational experiences per session with the boy; help the boy in his decision on how to earn the money to pay back his parents or church for the cost of the camping experience; and participate in the closing service of the program at the end of October.

The ideology of the Bailey Program is to encourage the boys to value their spiritual, mental, and physical beings. This type of personal advancement influences the intellectual development of the boys and enhances their attitudes towards life. The boys are then able to project this confidence within their community and serve as an example to other African American boys. The Rites of Passage Program for boys emphasizes to the youth the important relationship he maintains with his church, family, and African heritage.

The formula for the Bailey Program is based on the book *Bringing the Black Boy to Manhood: The Passage* by Nathan and Julia Hare (Black Think Tank, 1987). The program's activities exercise the main ideals of reidentification, reclarification, re-definition, and re-affirmation through the following techniques:

- Teaching positive relational skills.
- Disseminating vital and important information.
- Demonstrating and modeling responsible adulthood.
- Reidentifying roles and relationships in the African community.
- Educating the boys on the importance of culture, history, and the diversity of African American contributions to the world's development.

The Howard Bailey Life Enrichment Program for African American Boys is a model "conference-wide" rites-of-passage ministry that can be replicated in each conference of the United Methodist Church. This would serve to foster fellowship among churches that serve in a particular conference. It is also an excellent way of doing evangelism.

It Works!

The miracle of the Howard Bailey Life Enrichment Program is the pervasive transformation seen in the lives and experiences of the participating boys.

Rashauan Ford is a boy small of stature for his age but obviously gifted with leadership abilities. Prior to his becoming a "Bailey man," he was beginning to display negative acting-out behaviors in school and in the community. According to his mother, he seemed to be getting in trouble in school in new and puzzling ways. In hindsight, it seems obvious that Rashauan was crying out to have his leadership skills and insight taken seriously in a system (school and rural community) that was not responding favorably.

He is not merely a bright spot in this program, but he continues to provide insightful leadership with the boys and for the program. One particular noteworthy incident occurred on the final evening of the 1992 summer camp retreat. After a long day of activity, visiting Union Temple Baptist Church, the Frederick Douglass House, and Howard University in Washington, D.C., one of the boys asked what could he do to be a better boy. Before the program leaders could respond, Rashauan suggested the way to be better was to commit your life to God and to trust your leader in the Bailey Life Enrichment Program for boys. Now, after his participation in the 1993 program, Rashauan has had influence on his entire family. Not only does he speak in an outgoing and enthusiastic way about the program, but his family also is very cooperative and can speak at length about how he has matured.

Contact:

The Howard Bailey Life Enrichment Program
139 North State Street
Dover, Delaware 19901
(302) 674-2626

Appendix I

What Makes a Foundation Proposal Work?

America's foundations are a six-billion-dollar-a-year income source for charitable organizations. How does a nonprofit tap into this potential revenue? An important key is the proposal. Paving the way for a proposal and crafting it correctly can make the difference in whether your project is funded.

Before you approach a foundation, do some preliminary research. Identify foundations with grant interests that coincide with your work, geographic focus, and funding needs. You can research possibilities in special directories that list and describe local, state, and national foundations. To find them, check with your local library, community foundation, or charitable clearinghouse organization. The Foundation Directory, published annually by The Foundation Center, is a helpful resource. Based in New York City with branches and cooperating collections throughout the country, The Foundation Center collects and publishes information on private charitable giving.

Next, try to get to know some of the foundation's staff members. Request an annual report and grant application with the foundation's proposal guidelines, procedures, and grant-making calendar. (Plan ahead; some foundations take six months to make final decisions.)

Enlist people you know who have relationships with the foundation. Such contacts help make your application stand out from others. It's important to establish some relationship with a staff person before you submit a formal proposal; then let that contact know when your proposal is on its way.

The proposal itself usually should be no more than eight pages and should begin with a short, compelling summary that includes the project's cost and how much you are asking from the foundation.

The body should include:

- A need statement. What is the problem you are trying to solve?
- Your project's goals and objectives.
- Your organization's credentials.
- Your proposed methodology. What, specifically, are you going to do? Who will do the work? Are you working with other organizations?
- Evaluation. How will you know whether you're successful?
- Your budget. It should list as direct costs all expenses, such as salaries, fringe benefits, travel, postage, supplies, printing, phone, and administration, necessary to conduct the project. Although many funders are hesitant to support accounting services, fund-raising expenses, and overhead, list and label them under indirect costs.
- Be sure to include relevant news clips, brochures, and publications as well as your annual report, a list of your board members, and a copy of your 501(c)(3) letter.*

In a short cover letter, try to include an invitation to some upcoming event that could showcase or personalize your project. Call your contact to verify your proposal's arrival and follow up on your invitation.

If you are turned down, be gracious. Send a letter thanking the foundation for its consideration, but get back to your contact and find out whether your project might stand a chance in the future and what could improve that chance. Then reapply with a revised proposal based on what you learn.

If you receive funding, congratulations! Now, keep in touch. Funders like to hear from their grantees, and you may want renewed funding.

Foundations

The following is a partial listing of foundations that grant monies to churches for programs designed to help children and their families.

* A 501 (c) (3) is a nonprofit, tax-exempt organization, such as a church.

Lilly Endowment, Inc.
2801 North Meridian Street   Program Director, Religion
Indianapolis, IN 46208-0068   (317) 924-5471

Ford Foundation
320 East 43rd Street   Program Director
New York, NY 10017   Black Religious Affairs
(212) 573-5000

Pew Charitable Trust
One Commerce Square   Program Director
2005 Market Street, Suite 1700   (215) 575-4730
Philadelphia, PA 19103-7017

Piton Foundation
The Republic Plaza Building   Program Director
370 17th Street, Suite 5300   (303) 825-6246
Denver, CO 80202

Jessie Ball duPont
225 Water Street, Suite 1200   Program Director
Jacksonville, FL 32202-0890   (904) 353-0890

John A. Hartford Foundation, Inc.
55 East 59th Street   Program Director
New York, NY 10022   (212) 832-7788

San Francisco Community
Foundations
685 Market Street, Suite 910   Program Director
San Francisco, CA 94105   (415) 495-3100

Meyer Memorial Trust
1515 SW Fifth Avenue, Suite 500   Executive Director
Portland, OR 97201   (503) 228-5512

Godfrey M. Hyams Trust
One Boston Place, 32nd Floor   Program Director
Boston, MA 02108   (617) 720-2238

Appendix II

Resources

This is a partial list of resources that may be helpful for ministries with children and youth.

Children's Defense Fund

An Advocate's Guide to Fund Raising. The basics of how to raise money from foundations, corporations, and individuals. 1990.

Mounting a Prenatal Care Campaign in Your Community. How to collect, compile, and present information to make the case for expanded prenatal care services in your communty. 1986.

Progress and Peril: Black Children in America. This is a fact book and action primer that details the unacceptable odds facing black children and summons us all to action. 1993.

Prophetic Voices: Black Preachers Speak on Behalf of Children. A unique collection of sermons by twenty-one African American preachers representing thirteen denominations. 1993.

Welcome the Child: A Child Advocacy Guide for Churches. This guide describes how to involve the congregation in child advocacy, include children and their concerns in the congregation's worship and programming, and tap into national denominational programs for children. Revised and expanded, 1994.

Mentoring

Adebonojo, Mary. *Free to Choose: Youth Program Resources from the Black Experience.* Valley Forge, Pa.: Judson Press, 1980.

Fair, Frank T. *Orita for Black Youth: An Initiation into Chris-*

tian Adulthood, revised edition. Valley Forge: Judson Press, forthcoming.

Flaxman, E., C. Ascher, and C. Harrington. *Mentoring Programs and Practices: An Annotated Bibliography.* ERIC, 1988. Available from ERIC Clearinghouse on Urban Education, Box 40, Teachers College, Columbia University, New York, NY 10027, (212) 678-3433.

Mentoring Manual: A Guide to Program Development and the Two of Us: A Handbook for Mentors. Published by the Abell Foundation, Baltimore, Maryland. Available from the Baltimore Mentoring Institute, 605 North Eutaw Street, Baltimore, MD 21201, (410) 685-8316.

Shockley, Grant. *Working with Black Youth.* Nashville: Abingdon Press, 1989.

Child Care

A Place for Growing: Child Care in the Church. Thirty minute video, available for rental. Ecumenical Child Care Network. (1985).

Bredekanmp, S., ed., *Developmentally Appropriate Practice in Early Childhood Programs Serving Children from Birth Through Age 8.* (1987). Washington, D.C.: National Association for the Education of Young Children (NAEYC #224).

Freeman, Margery. *Called to Act: Stories of Child Care Advocacy in Our Churches.* New York: All Union Press, 1986.

Freeman, Margery., ed. *Helping Churches Mind the Children: A Guide for Church-Housed Child Day Care Programs.* New York: National Council of the Churches of Christ in the U.S.A., 1987.

Godwin, A., & Schrag, L. *Setting Up for Infant Care: Guidelines for Centers and Family Day Care Homes.* (1988). Washington, D.C.: National Association for the Education of Young Children (NAEYC #228).

Helping Churches Mind the Children, rev. ed. Ecumenical Child Care Network. (1987).

In the Eye of the Storm: Liability and Church Child Care. National Council of Churches Child Advocacy Resources. Ecumenical Child Care Network. (1988).

More Than 50 Nifty Ideas for Improving Church Child-Care

Program Relationships. Ecumenical Child Care Network. (1988).

Financial Assistance

How to Obtain Financial Assistance. National Academy of Early Childhood Programs. A fund-raising packet for early childhood programs. Washington, D.C.: National Association for the Education of Young Children.

Parent Networks

Allen, Mary Lee, Patricia Brown, and Belva Finlay. *Helping Children by Strengthening Families: A Look at Family Support Programs.* The Children's Defense Fund, 1992.

Boukydis, C.F.Z., ed. *Support for Parents and Infants.* New York: Routledge & Kegan Paul, 1986.

Garland, D.S.R., K.C. Chapman, and J. Pounds. *Parenting by Grace: Self-esteem.* A thirteen-session, biblically based, parent education program for use with a group of parents in a local church. Nashville: The Sunday School Board of the Southern Baptist Convention. 1990.

Houghton, E.W. *Organizing Parents into an Effective Prevention Network.* Informed Networks Inc., 200 Ramsey Road, Deerfield, IL, 1986.

Johns, Mary Lee. *Developing Church Programs to Prevent Child Abuse.* Austin: Texas Conference of Churches, 1988.

Levine, Carole, ed. *Programs to Strengthen Families: A Resource Guide.* Chicago: Family Resource Coalition, 1988.

General Resources

Clark, Tina. *Concern into Action: An Advocacy Guide for People of Faith.* 1990. Available from Interfaith IMPACT.

Comer, James P., and Alvin F. Poussaint, *Raising Black Children.* New York: Penguin Press, 1992.

Froland, C., et al. *Helping Networks and Human Services.* Beverly Hills, Calif.: Sage, 1981.

Garland, Diana S. Richmond, and Diane L. Pancoast, *The Church's Ministry with Families.* Dallas: Word Publishing Inc, 1990.

Hopson, Dr. Darlene Powell, and Dr. Derek S. Hopson. *Different and Wonderful: Raising Black Children in a Race-Conscious Society.* New York: Prentice Hall Press, 1990.

Joseph, M.V. *The Parish as a Ministering Community: Social Ministries in the Local Church Community.* Hyattsville, Md.: Pen Press, 1988.

Lakin, D., and J. Hargett. "The Role of the Black Church in the Adoption of Black Children with Developmental Disabilities." Paper presented to the NASW Clinical Social Work Conference, San Francisco, September 12, 1986.

Smith, Wallace Charles. *The Church in the Life of the Black Family.* Valley Forge: Judson Press, 1985.

Institutional Resources

Churchsteps: The African American Church Resource Guide. Howard University School of Divinity, Washington, D.C. Available from the H.U.D.S. Information and Services Clearinghouse at (202) 806-0750.

The Source. A free newsletter that promotes positive development of children and youth. The Search Institute, Thresher Square West, Suite 210, 700 South 3rd Street, Minneapolis, MN 55415, (800) 888-7828.

Appendix III

National Ecumenical/Denominational Efforts for Children

The Ecumenical Child Care
  Network (ECCN)
1580 North Northwest
Highway, #115
Park Ridge, IL 60068-1456
(708) 298-1612

The Ecumenical Child
  Health Project
National Council of Churches
475 Riverside Drive, Room 572
New York, NY 10115
(212) 870-2664

National Council of Churches
  Committee on Justice for
  Children and Their Families
475 Riverside Drive
New York, NY 10015
(212) 870-2511

Interfaith IMPACT for Justice
  and Peace
100 Maryland Avenue NE
Washington, DC 20002
(202) 543-2800

African Methodist Episcopal
  Church
Connectional Director,
  Young People's Division of
  the Women's Missionary
  Society
3194 Baxberry Court
Decatur, GA 30034-5102
(404) 284-7015

African Methodist Episcopal
  Zion Church
Christian Education
  Department
P.O. Box 32305
Charlotte, NC 28231
(704) 332-9323

American Baptist Churches
  in the U.S.A.
Department of Education for
  Discipleship
Educational Ministries
P.O. Box 851
Valley Forge, PA 19482-0851
(215) 768-2000

Christian Church (Disciples
  of Christ)
Children's Ministries
Division of Homeland
  Ministries
P.O. Box 1986
Indianapolis, IN 46206-1986
(317) 353-1499

Christian Methodist
  Episcopal Church
4466 Elvis Presley
Boulevard, Suite 214
Box 193
Memphis, TN 38116
(901) 345-0580

Church of God
Children and Family
  Ministries
P.O. Box 2458
Anderson, IN 46018-2458
(800) 848-2464

Church of God
Youth & Christian Education
P.O. Box 2430
Cleveland, TN 37320
(615) 472-3361

Church of God in Christ
Department of Youth
260 Roydon Road
New Haven, CT 06511

The Episcopal Church
Office of Children's
  Ministries
815 Second Avenue
New York, NY 10017

(212) 922-5264

Evangelical Lutheran Church
  in America
Division for Congregational
  Ministries
Child Advocacy
8765 West Higgins Road
Chicago, IL 60631
(312) 380-2700

National Baptist Convention,
  U.S.A., Inc.
Women's Auxiliary
  Convention
584 Arden Pike
Detroit, MI 48202
(313) 872-7155

National Baptist Convention
  of America
777 S.R.L. Thornton
Freeway, Suite 205
Dallas, TX 75203
(214) 946-8913

Presbyterian Child Advocacy
  Network of the Presbyterian
  Health, Education and
  Welfare Association
100 Witherspoon Street
Louisville, KY 40202-1396
(502) 569-5800

Progressive National Baptist
  Convention
601 50th Street NE
Washington, DC 20019
(202) 396-0558

Roman Catholic Church
Catholic Charities USA
1731 King Street, Suite 200
Alexandria, VA 22314
(703) 549-1390

Outreach Director
Department of Social
  Development and World
  Peace
U.S. Catholic Conference
The Catholic Campaign for
  Children & Family
3211 Fourth Street NE
Washington, DC 20017
(202) 541-3195

Seventh-Day Adventist
  Church
12501 Old Columbia Pike
Silver Spring, MD
20904-6600
(301) 680-6000

Southern Baptist Convention
Child Advocacy Network
Southern Baptist Theological
  Seminary
2825 Lexington Road
Louisville, KY 40280
(800) 626-5525
(502) 897-4607

United Church of Christ
United Church Board for
  Homeland Ministries
Secretary for Human
  Development, Programs and
  Concerns

700 Prospect Avenue East.
Cleveland, OH 44115
(216) 736-3282

United Methodist Church
Children, Youth and Family
  Advocacy
Women's Division
475 Riverside Drive, Room
  1502
New York, NY 10115
(212) 870-3766

Office of Children's
  Ministries
General Board of Discipleship
P.O. Box 840
Nashville, TN 37202-0840
(615) 340-7171

Unitarian Universalist
  Association
Unitarian Universalist
  Service Committee, Inc.
Promise the Children
78 Beacon Street
Boston, MA 02108
(617) 742-2100

Appendix IV

Faith-Based Public Policy Offices and National Organizations

Ecumenical Organizations

Churches' Center for
  Theology and Public Policy
4500 Massachusetts Avenue,
NW
Washington, DC 20016
(202) 885-8648

Church Women United
Washington Office:
110 Maryland Avenue, NE
Washington, DC 20002
(202) 544-8747

New York Office:
475 Riverside Drive, Room
  812
New York, NY 10115-0050
(212) 870-2347

The Congress of National
  Black Churches
1225 Eye Street, NW, Suite
  750
Washington, DC 20005
(202) 371-1091

Ecumenical Child Care
  Network
1580 North Northwest
  Highway, #115
Park Ridge, IL 60068-1456
(708) 298-1612

Interfaith IMPACT for Justice
  & Peace
100 Maryland Avenue NE
Washington, DC 20002
(202) 543-2800

The National Council of the
  Churches of Christ in the
  U.S.A.
Washington Office:
110 Maryland Avenue NE
Washington, DC 20002
(202) 544-2350

Denominational Public Policy Offices

American Baptist Churches,
  USA
Office of Governmental
  Relations

110 Maryland Avenue NE,
  Suite 511
Washington, DC 20002
(202) 544-3400

Christian Church (Disciples
  of Christ)
Center for Education and
  Mission
222 South Downey Avenue
Indianapolis, IN 46206
(317) 353-1491, ext. 374

The Episcopal Church
Washington Office:
110 Maryland Avenue NE
Washington, DC 20002
(202) 547-7300
(800) 228-0515

Episcopal Church Public
  Policy Network
Public Ministries Cluster
The Episcopal Church Center
815 Second Avenue
New York, NY 10017
(212) 867-8400
(800) 334-7626

Evangelical Lutheran Church
  in America
Office for Governmental
  Affairs
122 C Street NW, Suite 300
Washington, DC 20001
(202) 783-7507

NETWORK: A National
  Catholic Social Justice Lobby
806 Rhode Island Avenue NE

Washington, DC 20018
(202) 526-4070

Presbyterian Church (USA)
110 Maryland Avenue NE,
Box 52
Washington, DC 20002
(202) 543-1126

Unitarian Universalist
  Association of Congregations
  (UUA)
100 Maryland Avenue NE,
#106
Washington, DC 20002
(202) 387-4587

United Church of Christ
  (UCC)
Office of Church in Society
110 Maryland Avenue NE
Washington, DC 20002
(202) 543-1517

United Methodist Church
General Board of Church and
  Society
100 Maryland Avenue NE
Washington, DC 20002
(202) 488-5660

General Board of Global
  Ministries
Women's Division
475 Riverside Drive, Room
  1502
New York, NY 10115
(212) 870-3766

General Board of Discipleship
Division of Educational
  Ministries
PO Box 840
Nashville, TN 37212-0840
(615) 340-7171

National Organizations

Bread for the World
1100 Wayne Avenue
Silver Spring, MD 20910
(301) 608-2400

Child Welfare League of
  America
440 First Street NW, Suite
  310
Washington, DC 20001
(202) 638-2952

Children's Defense Fund
25 E Street NW
Washington, DC 20001
(202) 628-8787

Food Research and Action
  Center (FRAC)
1875 Connecticut Avenue
  NW, Suite 540
Washington, DC 20009
(202) 986-2200

Habitat for Humanity
  International
121 Habitat Street
Americus, GA 31709
(912) 924-6935

National Association for the
  Education of Young Children
1509 16th Street NW
Washington, DC 20036
(202) 232-8777

National Black Child
  Development Institute
1463 Rhode Island Avenue
  NW
Washington, DC 20005
(202) 387-1281